GW01086449

When God Invades Your Everyday Life

Practical Day-to-Day Experiences
With God
A Weekly Devotional

Donald E Honig

DEDICATION

To my wife, Norma, who has encouraged and believed that I had the makings of a book inside me, a great big thank you for your patience, and to my many church friends here in the states, as-well-as in Israel and Germany who have provided a base of support, encouragement, and intercession for the journey which at long last has become a reality.

Contents

Introduction

Ever since I became a believer in the Lord Jesus Christ, I have been amazed how God moved supernaturally in my natural surroundings. It could be walking by a swimming pool or driving a car or even during a trans-Atlantic flight. God has always made His presence known to me.

When I was a young believer, I thought that as a Holy God, He would only reveal himself in special places like a church building or a tent meeting, but the idea that God could and would manifest His presence in something like a supermarket or a walk in the park was beyond my understanding.

As I began to read scripture, it became very clear to me that not only could God manifest Himself wherever He wanted to, but that He would intimately get involved in every aspect of my life as He did with Abraham, Isaac and Jacob, as-well-as common people that had a heart for the deeper things of God.

I was equally amazed that God would also introduce himself in such a way that He would knock you off your horse as He did with Paul in the New Covenant, knowing fully well that Paul wasn't even looking for God.

This book is a journal of God invading my everyday comings and goings and how He speaks to me through normal, day-by-day experiences and shows me that the heart of God is a heart of love for each and every child of God.

This book represents a 52 week devotional, and at the end of each devotion, there is a simple prayer and a few questions that I would encourage you to reflect on and answer in your own words.

My prayer for you the reader is that you will not only begin to expect God to reveal Himself to you, but will manifest His presence in everything you do and every place you go, and that you will hear His voice in the silence around you and see His face always looking back at you with those reassuring words that He will never leave you nor forsake you.

Week 1
A Simple Package of Dried Chicken Noodle Soup

I want to share with you something the Lord revealed to me the day after I cooked a simple meal, and this mini sharing has everything to do with the cooking and if taken internally, it can change your life forever.

As many of you know, I love to cook and even consider myself to be pretty good at it; I mean after all, I've been doing it for over 50 years, so I should know something about it.

It was dinner time and I was in the mood for some soup, but the only thing I had was one of those real simple packages of dry chicken noodle soup. You know the type, you add water and wait and hope the rock hard noodles have softened and you eat it thinking of what real soup must taste like.

Anyway, I thought to myself, 'Why don't you kind of doctor this up'. So I found some real potatoes and carrots and took a few pieces of fresh dark meat chicken that I had just purchased and cut all the ingredients into small cubes and added it all to the soup mix. I found some seasoning and added that, thereafter, I covered it and let it simmer after bringing it to a boil.

In 30 minutes, I removed the lid and tasted the soup and WOW! It was excellent. It was so good that I didn't want to share it, but thought it would be nice if Norma had some of this wonderful soup. She tried it and really liked it also.

1

Part of me was saying it's good, but it's not "real" chicken soup. Another part of me was saying; if it looks like a duck, quacks like a duck and walks like a duck, it must be a duck. Well, this looked like chicken soup, smelled like chicken soup and tasted like chicken soup, so it must be chicken soup.

I thought this was too easy. That's when the Lord spoke to me the next day at the breakfast table.

He brought to my remembrance a story I heard many years ago about an estate auction where everything went up on the selling block. At last, it came to a very old and dusty violin, and the auctioneer opened with a bid of $100.00. No one bid on the violin, so the auctioneer reduced the bid to $75.00. Still no one bid on this old violin, so again the bid was reduced to $50.00. At this time, a very old gentleman walked up to the violin and placed it under his chin and began to play the most amazing, incredible music. It was like liquid gold pouring forth from the violin, and the crowd was in a stunned silence as they listened to this music. When done, the old man handed the violin back to the auctioneer and walked away. With that, the auctioneer began the bid again starting at $10,000. Someone asked him, why the jump in the price, what changed? To which the auctioneer responded; it was the hands of the Master.

You might be asking; "What does this have to do with the cooking story"? Well, the simplest ingredients in the hands of the master can transform a package of dried chicken noodle soup into a wonderful meal. Don't get me wrong, I am no master, just a simple cook that loves cooking.

This is what the Lord showed me: Often times, we look at our lives and think we could never do this or never do that. I have no formal training. I could never speak in front of all those people, I'm too shy or I get too nervous, or I might forget what it is I'm supposed to say.

The key word in all these situations is "I". I can't, I could never, I might, etc. Guys, it's not about "I". We are surely nothing but ingredient in the hands of The Master.

Psalm 118:23. "The LORD has done this, and it is marvelous in our eyes."

Psalm 126:3. "The LORD has done great things for us, and we are filled with joy."

Psalm 111:2. " Great are the works of The Lord, and they are sought out by all who desire them."

We are all aware it is not our great abilities, but our availabilities that The Master is looking for and able to use.

For example in **Acts 4:13**, it tells us "but seeing the boldness of Peter and John, and perceiving that they were unlearned and uneducated men, they marveled. And they recognized them that they had been with Jesus."

Another version puts it this way: "When they saw the courage of Peter and John and realized that they were unschooled, ordinary men, they were astonished and they took note that these men had been with Jesus."

That word unlearned means: "those who were not acquainted with letters, or who had not had the benefit of an education."

3

You see, John and Peter were like that package of dried chicken noodle soup. Nothing special, but with the Lord adding His special touch, they left a mark on the people who heard them speak.

Any if you are young, don't let that be a hindrance because you can also leave an impression or mark on everyone around you. We are told in **I Timothy 4:12**, "don't let anyone look down on you for being young. Instead, make your speech, behavior, love, faith, and purity an example for other believers."

Every one of us leaves our fingerprints on the lives of other people, especially on our children.

We don't stay on earth forever; but after we're gone, our imprint remains. How many times have you remembered what someone did in your life although you don't remember what they said? And this applies to good and not so good actions.

According to Christian Biography Resources, one example is of John Geddie, Canadian missionary to the New Hebrides. He found a tribe of cannibals. Violence, theft, and warfare were common.

After he died, a commemorative tablet in his island church read: "In memory of John Geddie. . . . When he landed in 1848, there were no Christians here, and when he left in 1872, there were no heathen."

How often have we said "Lord, use me"? He has never said to us, "I can't, you need more training". Instead, He tells us in **James 4:2b**, "you don't have what you want because you don't ask God for it". And again in **John**

4

16:24, we are told "until now you have not asked for anything in my name. Ask and you will receive it, that your joy may be perfect."

The enemy wants us to keep our eyes on ourselves and our short comings, and focus on 'the cannot' while Jesus wants us to put our eyes on Him and focus on the 'can'. For example in **Matthew 14:29**, we are told "Jesus said, "Come on!" So Peter got down out of the boat, started walking on the water, and came to Jesus." Peter asked for something in His name and received it and his joy was full, imagine just like **John 16:24**, told us. It couldn't happen until Peter took his eyes off the winds, waves and what will likely happen to him, and then, put them on the Lord. Jesus is the Rock and unshakable fortress so if we are in Him, the shakable wind and waves have to become silent.

I said all that to say this: sometimes, we may feel like mere dried out ingredients just prodding our way through life, but in the hands of The Master, He can transform the ordinary into the extraordinary, the credible into the incredible and the 'OW' into a 'WOW'. You just need to let Him do what He does best, change lives by adding more of Him to us and taking away from us what is not of Him.

And sometimes, the hot water is needed to soften the hard noodles and dried ingredients of our lives, but the final outcome won't look anything like what you look like now.

Prayer: Lord, help me to believe that although I'm far from being perfect, you can still use me to make a difference in the Kingdom of God for Your glory.

1. What do you think is more pleasing to the Lord; each individual ingredient or the final outcome of all the ingredients combined?
2. Why do you think it's more important for the Lord to reveal the ingredients than for us to choose the ingredients based on our years of experience in preparation?

Week 2
An Anchor That Holds

Ever have one of those moments that you inadvertently see something that you weren't looking for and it jumps out at you and speaks to your spirit? Like a colorful sunset or a sky filled with stars or anything that triggers your spirit to be thankful for being alive and that God is in control.

Well, it happened to me the other day when I was looking at Norma's computer and I noticed she had a screen saver quote by Augustine that said "God is not a deceiver that He should offer to help and support us, and then, when we lean upon Him, should slip away from us."

It brings to my remembrance **Psalms 54:4**, "Behold, God is my helper. The Lord is the one who sustains my soul," and **Psalms 94:17**, "If the Lord had not been my helper, my soul would quickly have gone down into death."

I'm so thankful that not only is God good, but He is faithful to a thousand generations, and so intimately involved in my life, but when He said I will never leave you nor forsake you, He actually meant every word of it. It causes me to stretch my imagination as to what it means to never leave or forsake anything. As humans, I believe we tend to leave things as soon as we grow tired of them or lose interest in them. It would seem if we are not entertained by something, then it holds no interest to us.

The word forsake according to Encarta Dictionary, means to withdraw companionship, protection, or support and according to Bing, it means to renounce or turn away from entirely.

So what did God actually say? Well, He said; "I will never withdraw companionship, protection or support from you nor will I ever renounce or turn away from you entirely." I don't know about you, but that is quite a promise, and only God has the ability and power to keep that promise, after all, He is not a man that He should ever lie to us.

Listen to these promises made by the Lord Himself.

I Kings 8:57 says, "May the LORD our God be with us, as He was with our fathers; May He not leave us or forsake us."

Hebrews 13:5 also confirms that when it tells us: Keep your life free from love of money, and be content with what you have, for he has said, "I will never leave you nor forsake you."

Deuteronomy 31:8 says, "The LORD himself goes before you and will be with you; he will never leave you nor forsake you. Do not be afraid; do not be discouraged."

Why am I so thankful? Because When God said He would never forsake me and would be my Helper, it was an unconditional promise, meaning, it had nothing to do with my behavior or performance or based upon what I did or said. What does that mean? It means that when I'm going through times of doubt or feelings of being alone or self-imposed thoughts of rejection and failure, He is still there. It's nice when you can feel His presence, but we are not to live by feelings, although, we can't deny that we have them. But what happens when you can't feel His presence

8

and you are walking in that valley of the shadow of death season in your life? Truth be told, He is still there and just a prayer away.

Of course, this also means that there are times that I take the Lord into situations or places that He would rather not be or subject Him to words or thoughts He would rather not hear. You see my friends; there is a price we have to pay for an unconditional promise of the Lord. This is why Paul tells us in **Acts 24:16**, "because of this belief, I always do my best to have a clear conscience in the sight of God and people". That word conscience according to Bing means: the inner sense of what is right or wrong in one's conduct or motives, impelling one toward right action.

So back to Augustine's incredible statement of: "God is not a deceiver or one who misleads by false appearance or statement that He should offer to help and support us, and then, when we lean upon Him, should slip away from us."

What did Augustine actually tell us? Well, with your permission, I'm taking the liberty of paraphrasing it, but he said that; God is not one who would mislead us with His words when He said I will never leave you nor forsake you and will always be there when you need Me or just want to talk. I will be more than just a listening ear and a presence, but I will be there for every need you will ever have and I have the authority and the power to accomplish that and when you do come to Me at any time, at any place for any reason, I won't be busy doing something else or put you on hold when you call, I will give you 100% of My undivided attention. I desire to help you more than you often times desire to be helped, and the advice and help that I provide is exactly what you need for the situation. Even if you lean on Me before you make any decisions, I will lead you and guide you to exactly what needs to be done because "I know the plans that I have for you," declares the LORD, "plans to prosper you and not to harm you, plans to give you hope and a future." I revealed that to My prophet, Jeremiah, and I'm revealing that to each and every one of you.

Knowing that, my friends, we are truly a blessed people because we have such a wonderful, loving, caring God.

Prayer: Lord, help me to see you with the eyes of my heart when I don't feel your presence and the darkness is all around me.

1. The same way that you cannot see the stars when there's a heavy overcast, how do you know that God is present when you don't feel His presence?
2. Have you ever abandoned a project or given up on a direction in life that you were following only to find it was the right direction all the time? How did it make you feel?

Week 3
Don't Let the Enemy Steal Your Happy Thoughts

The Lord woke me up one early morning and asked me a question. 'Have you allowed the enemy to steal your happy thoughts'?

As I pondered on this question, I was reminded of a movie called Hook with Robin Williams and Dustin Hoffman. In the movie, there's a scene that spoke to me. It was where the son, Jack, an 11 year old who was very disappointed in his dad for not sticking up for him and never being there for him. Jack was finally won over by Captain Hook, the villain because he promised to be there for him all the time. In this scene, Jack was playing baseball, his favorite sport and hits the ball which goes out of sight, obviously a home run. As he starts around the bases, the cheer leading team which is made up of pirates, holds up signs that say, 'Run Home Jack.' For a moment, Jack's happy thought was of home and he hesitates. The cheer leading pirates are corrected of their mistake and change the signs to read 'Home Run Jack,' and the happy thought is gone, and once again, Jack forgets home and gets on with the game.

You know the things that we sometimes think about can either bring us joy, pain, anger and often incredible amounts of stress. And many of the negative things we sometimes think about have often happened years and years ago, but we have not learned to let them go. In other words, what we think about can affect our daily life and walk with God. This is why in **Philippian's 4:8,** it tells us in the Aramaic Bible in the Plain English version

11

"Therefore, my brethren, those things that are true, those that are honorable, those that are righteous, those things that are pure, those things that are precious, those things that are praiseworthy, deeds of glory and of praise, think on these things."

And in the GOD'S WORD® Translation;

"Finally, brothers and sisters, keep your thoughts on whatever is right or deserves praise: things that are true, honorable, fair, pure, acceptable, or commendable."

Sometimes, it would almost seem that the things that we think upon have a mind of their own and the negative ones seem to always present themselves in the night when we are trying to go to sleep.

Have you ever tried to go to sleep, only to have a thought keep you wide awake? It can be a thought of a coming interview, a meeting or a school final exam, or a thought of someone who wronged you five years ago, and as hard as you try to put it out of your mind, it comes back just as strongly. As a matter of fact, you try really hard to think on something else that will bring you peace, and hopefully sleep. It would almost seem that you have no choice on what you are able to think upon.

I say almost because here's the good news, you do have a choice. According to **Psalms 63:6**, it tells us "As I lie on my bed, I remember you. Through the long hours of the night, I think about you."

In other words, although the enemy is trying to steal your happy thought, you have the power to choose what you will think about, and what you think about will affect your life.

12

Psalms 1:2 tells us, "But his delight is in the law of the LORD, and on his law, he thinks day and night."

If what you think about doesn't bring you peace of mind or closer to God, I believe you need to think about something else. Personally speaking, I haven't found anything harder than changing my thoughts in mid-stream. It's like a battle going on in my mind. Sometimes, when I have a mind battle over something that I know is so, and I can't think of a better word, STUPID. It almost seems impossible to switch. I mean it's not like turning a light on and off. So what do I do? I work hard at focusing on **Philippians 4:8**, "Finally, brothers and sisters, keep your thoughts on whatever is right or deserves praise: things that are true, honorable, fair, pure, acceptable, or worthy of praise."

No one said it was easy. But what I do know is that; it's not impossible.

And you know, the world doesn't help. That's why I try to commit that verse to memory, realizing that what society has to offer today is the exact opposite. Look at the TV listings, the popular magazines, even our newspapers, and you will often see glorification of things that are impure, wrong and untrue. People focus so much on the negative that the media seldom features positive news because they're afraid they'll lose their audience.

Titus 1:10 in a particular translation, he uses a word that really describes what the things of this world are, he calls them "mind-deceivers". If we think upon those things, we lose our peace and joy, and obviously our sweet sleep because our minds have been deceived. But if we think upon the things of God, we gain peace and joy because as **2**

13

Thessalonians 3:16 tells us: "Now may the Lord of peace himself give you peace at all times and in every way."

I encourage you, think upon the things that the Lord has done and rest in knowing that the steps of the righteous are ordered of the Lord and that truly all things will work out for the better as you give Him the control of your life.

Prayer: Lord, really search me and try me, and if there is anything that is not pleasing to You, remove it from me so I can get closer to you.

1. Have you ever lost your happy thought because your pride got in the way, and you knew it was your pride? How did that make you feel as a child of God?
2. When the enemy tries to steal your happy thought, how do you press in to the deeper things of God to overcome the enemies' attempt to steal from you?

Week 4
Exceedingly, Abundantly

The other day I was meditating on two words, exceedingly, and the word, abundantly. I found according to the dictionary that exceedingly means to an extreme degree, and abundantly means, according to the same Bing dictionary, to be present in great quantity or plentiful.

Most of the time, we find one or the other of these words, but when it comes to the provisions of God towards His children, and by the way; that's me and you, we find in **Ephesians 3:20,** "Now to him that is able to do exceeding abundantly above all that we ask or think, according to the power that works in us." Another version says it this way: "Now to Him who, in exercise of His power that is at work within us, is able to do infinitely beyond all our highest prayers or thoughts."

In other words, whatever it is that we can think up or pray about has a basis, which is based on the power of God which is not only working in us, but that power is present in great quantity to an extreme degree and is able to do infinitely way beyond all our highest prayers or thoughts.

There may be a shortage of things in the world, but let me say this, there is no shortage of God's power at work in us. Not only is it there, but it's there in great quantity to an extreme degree.

We use the words exceedingly abundantly, but did you know it is impossible to fully express the meaning of these words? Why? Because God is omnipotent, therefore, he is able to do all things, and able to do according to the Greek (ὑπερ εκ περισσου), superabundantly above the greatest abundance. This causes my head to spin.

Here's an example of exceedingly abundantly in action. In **Galatians 1:3,** it tells us; Grace to you and peace from God, the Father and our Lord Jesus Christ. To have grace and peace from God, the Father would be more than I could ever ask or imagine, but it tells me I have grace and peace from God, the Father and our Lord Jesus Christ. Talk about grace and peace in great quantity to an extreme degree, and all of that is ours.

So what did this all just tell us? We have according to Bing; the infinite love, mercy, favor, and goodwill of God, the Father and of Jesus Christ, in addition to the Shalom of God and Jesus Christ or a state of harmony characterized by the lack of violent conflict and the freedom from fear of violence, and we have that exceedingly abundantly more than we could have ever asked or imagined.

Are we blessed or what? In less than one sentence, we have received a spontaneous, unmerited gift of divine favor and a state of harmony characterized by the lack of violent conflict, commonly understood as the absence of hostility.

Getting bent out of shape or becoming a nervous wreck over things is not for us, we have all we need to last us a thousand life times and all because of "Him who, in exercise of His power that is at work within us, is able to do infinitely beyond all our highest prayers or thoughts."

Prayer: Father, help me to be content when I enter seasons of much or seasons of little, knowing that You are the giver of all good gifts.

1. If God truly directs our footsteps, why do we get so bent out of shape when He directs us in periods of need and want? Do you think it's a pride issue?
2. What do you think the expression means: Our Christian walk is sometimes like a roller coaster ride?

Week 5
Freedom

"So, if the Son sets you free, you will be free indeed." (Not my favorite translation). Another version says it this way: "So, if the Son sets you free, you are truly free." Better, but still not my favorite. My favorite version puts it this way: "So if the Son sets you free, you will be absolutely free."

The expression, 'will be' often gives the impression of its coming and truly hints at a very good possibility, but absolutely means; without exception; completely; wholly; entirely, certainly and without question.

There are three words in this verse that actually go hand-in-hand. Not only that, but if you remove any one of these three words, the entire sentence falls apart. These are the words; Son, absolutely and free.

If you remove the Son, not only are you not free, but you are still in darkness and absolutely in bondage to sin. Because there's only one who has the ability to forgive sin.

If you remove the word absolutely, it means you have a temporary victory over sin in a particular situation, but are still in bondage.

And if you remove the word free, I have no idea what the Son would have set you absolutely from. It's like you asking me "How are you today Don? And I tell you; "Brother, I am absolutely". Your next question is obvious, "absolutely WHAT?" I'm absolutely, absolutely.

18

So the next question now becomes, The Son has absolutely set us free from what? From paying taxes, working, supporting your family, obeying the law, getting older? Of course not, Christ didn't die on the cross so you wouldn't have to pay taxes or quit working or any of those things.

I heard a story about some chickens walking in circles around a pole. They had strings attached to their legs, and they continued to walk around and around the pole hour after hour, day after day. A man came into the market and asked, "How much will you take for all of them?" He paid the owner the agreed upon price and then began to cut the strings off of their legs.

"What are you doing?" the owner asked in disbelief?

"I'm setting them free," said the new owner. But in spite of the strings being cut giving the chickens their freedom, they continued to walk around the pole in the same old circle. They didn't even realize that they were free and that they could go in a different direction.

Let me say this; many in our society today are clueless as to what freedom is. Many think that freedom means, that they are free to do whatever they want - whenever they want. This Is Not Freedom.

In the name of freedom, millions of unborn are murdered each year, and what do they call it? Freedom of choice. Pornography fills the magazine racks and movie screens, and what do they call that? Freedom of speech... Cults are on the increase, all forms of magic is practiced, the physic network increases daily, satan is worshipped and what do they call that? Freedom of religion.

Jesus says, "If the Son sets you free, you are absolutely free indeed." Knowing that, we need to realize that we are absolutely free today from all kinds of things because of the Son freeing us. We need to go in a different direction. We don't have to continue to march around in the circles of guilt, sin, shame and condemnation.

We are free indeed. We use the word 'indeed' but do you really know what it means. It means; in fact; in reality; in truth; truly and is used for emphasis, to confirm and amplify a previous statement.

What's the previous statement or word? FREE! So if the Son sets you free, you are in fact, in reality, in truth, truly free.

If you have been set free, then, you are in freedom. What does that include?

Freedom from the Guilt of Sin: Sometimes, we walk around like the cartoon of the guy with a big, dark cloud of guilt or shame hanging over our heads because we are guilty of a sin that we committed recently or a long time ago.

Here's an example of a letter sent in to the IRS:

Gentlemen:

Enclosed, you will find a check for $150. I cheated on my income tax return last year and have not been able to sleep ever since. If I still have trouble sleeping, I will send you the rest.

Sincerely,

A Tax Payer

That person was not experiencing freedom.

Scripture tells us in **1 John 1:9** that, "if we confess our sins, he is faithful and just to forgive us our sins and to cleanse us from all unrighteousness." He takes care of our true guilt, but He also takes care of our false guilt. Sometimes, we have a more difficult time with the false guilt than we do with true guilt. Many Christians will say, "I feel guilty because I'm not good enough or I feel like I don't live up to what I think I ought to be or should do. I feel guilty because of (you fill in the blanks). What happens is that they are living under a cloud of condemnation (to express an unfavorable or negative judgment or to indicate a strong disapproval) and often it's aimed right at ourselves.

Scripture says in **Romans 8:1**, "Therefore, there is now no condemnation for those who are in Christ Jesus because through Christ Jesus the law of the Spirit of life set me free from the law of sin and death." The Message Bible puts it this way, "Those who enter Christ's being here-for-us no longer have to live under a continuous, low-lying black cloud. A new power is in operation. The Spirit of life in Christ, like a strong wind, has magnificently cleared the air, freeing you from a fated lifetime of a brutal harsh power at the hands of sin and death."

What has the Son set us free from? One of the biggest things that He has set us free from is the guilt of sin.

What else? Well, He has set us free from the Consequences of Sin: The truth is, much of the time, we have to suffer the consequences of our actions and we can't go back and erase the results of our actions. Example, sometimes, Norma will say something that is incorrect and when I bring it to her attention, she will often tell me; "just erase that." Wouldn't that be nice if we could just erase the issues that we are sorry about and they would be as if they never happened?

Let's be real, sometimes, we can't always just "fix" things. Parents often want to fix problems for their children because they don't want them to have to go through pain and suffering. Sin has consequences. **Romans 6:23** says, "The wages of sin is death, but the gift of God is eternal life in Christ Jesus our Lord." We can be free from the final consequence of sin through God's gift of eternal life.

What else has He set us free from? The Son has set us free to be all that God wants us to be: It's not just an army slogan, 'be all that you can be'; it's a reality that the Lord has for His children.

Galatians 5:16 tells us to "walk under the control of the Spirit and we will no longer be forced to live in bondage to the desires of the flesh." We no longer have to live angry, jealous, hateful, selfish, under guilt and condemnation or any other of the characteristics of a sinful lifestyle.

So two big questions are:

Are you free? If you are a believer, the answer is yes, are you walking in that freedom? You can be.

Remember **John 8:36**. "So if the Son, that's Jesus Christ, the Messiah sets you completely; wholly; entirely, certainly and without question free from the guilt of sin, the consequences of sin and to be all that God wants you to be, then you will be completely, wholly and absolutely free from the guilt of sin, from the consequences of sin and to be all that God wants you to be."

Only you can choose to walk in the freedom that is already yours or you can continue to walk in the guilt of past sins in your life.

Prayer: Lord, you truly set me free; help me to walk in that freedom daily and not to go back to the bondage that makes me a prisoner to every, and all things.

1. When the Lord tells us He set us free, do you think that's a permanent freedom or a temporary freedom and why do you think that?
2. What do you believe that you have been set free from?
3. Do you really believe that you are free, and does your life reflect that freedom?
4. What are you free from and what are you a slave to? How can you break that bondage to slavery?

Week 6
Transition from Servant to Friend

I was reading in **John 15:15** the other day, where it tells us: "No longer do I call you servants, because a servant does not know what his master does, but I have called you my friends, because all that I have heard from my Father, I have taught you."

Bing Dictionary tells me that a servant is a person employed by another, especially to perform domestic duties or a person in the service of another. *Encarta Dictionary* puts it this way: a servant is an employee who serves somebody else, especially an employee hired to do household tasks or be a personal attendant to somebody.

The bottom line is, a master doesn't have to or need to share deep things with a servant. In the Greek, a servant is considered to be a bond slave. Interestingly enough, according to HELPS Word-Studies, a bond slave is properly, someone who belongs to another without any ownership rights of their own. As strange as that may sound, a "bond-slave" is used with the highest dignity in the NT – namely, of believers who willingly live under Christ's authority as His devoted followers.

But Jesus said I no longer call you servants, but friends. According to Urban Dictionary, a friend is someone you love and who loves you, someone you respect and who respects you, someone whom you trust and who trusts you. A friend is honest and makes you want to be honest, too. A friend is loyal.

A friend is someone who tries to help you even when they don't know how. A friend is someone who would sacrifice their life and happiness for you.

A friend is someone for whom you're willing to change your opinions. A friend is someone you look forward to seeing and who looks forward to seeing you: someone you like so much, it doesn't matter if you share interests or traits. A friend is someone you like so much; you start to like the things they like.

What was it that caused Jesus to go from servant to friend? There had to be something that brought about this transition. If we look at the second part of the verse again, it tells us: "but I have called you my friends, because all that I have heard from my Father, I have taught you."

The word "because" is critical. In other words, I do this because of that. What was it that caused Jesus to go from servant to friend? It was because He heard something from the Father and He taught it to us.

You know, we live in an era with instant coffee, instant homes, and wanting instant results, but there is no such thing as a meaningful instant relationship. The key is time.

A teaching of liberation from the Father being taught by the Son caused a transition from servant to friend. But it's much deeper than that because learning from the Master means taking time, and that translates to relationship.

If we spend enough time with the Lord, it changes us. We transition from a person in the service of another to someone who loves us, someone who respects us, someone who trusts us.

25

All because the word of the Father taught by the Son over a period of time has changed us and it's all because of a relationship.

My friends, I encourage you to have the desire to spend the time with the Lord God Almighty, our friend and allow Him to teach you the words that He gets from the Father. The word of God will transition you from servant to friend, and according to **Proverbs 18:24,** "A man of many companions may come to ruin, but there is a friend who sticks closer than a brother, and that friend has a name and that name is Jesus, our friend."

Prayer: Lord, I know that I am Your friend and no longer Your servant. Help me to process that from my head to my heart so I can walk freely in that friendship relationship.

1. How is a relationship with a friend different than a relationship with a servant?
2. What freedom with the Lord does a friend have that a servant does not have?
3. In a world of instant everything, do you believe that you can establish an instant relationship with the Lord? Which would have a stronger bond, instant or timely?

Week 7
Give Credit Where Credit Is Due

The other night while I was sleeping, I heard a voice and it said; 'give credit where credit is due'. Half asleep and half awake, I said what? Again the voice said, 'give credit where credit is due'.

About this time, I was rather wide awake and I also knew who the voice was because I have heard it often, so I asked the question, Lord, what does give credit where credit is due actually mean?

You know the Lord is really wonderful in not answering direct questions and He said to me; "I have many names but gut-feeling, coincidence and hunch is not one of them.

I remember saying, 'Well, I know that'. God responded by saying "When I intervene in your life, I would like you to give the credit where the credit is due". I mean a simple 'thank you Lord' isn't too much trouble now, is it? Being wide away at this time, I decided to check out what God was saying to me about intervention.

In **Psalm 109:21** it tells us: "O sovereign Lord, intervene on my behalf for the sake of your reputation! Because your loyal love is good, deliver me!"

Psalm 20:6 tells us; "now I am sure that the Lord will deliver his chosen king; he will intervene for him from his holy heavenly temple, and display his mighty ability to deliver."

Just a few more.

27

Isaiah 30: 30 tells us; "The Lord will give a mighty shout and intervene in power…"

Jeremiah 14:7 says; "Then I said, 'O Lord, intervene for the honor of your name even though our sins speak out against us.' "

According to Dictionary.com, intervene means to intercede or to mediate or to come between.

As I was thinking about what God was showing me, it brought to my remembrance two incidents that were perfect examples of God's intervention in our lives.

One example took place in France when we landed at the main airport in Paris, which by the way is like a city in a city. Anyway, we were supposed to meet someone at a particular door and he was going to take us to where we needed to go. Here we were with three very large suitcases, two carry-ons and in a large airport completely lost. We had no idea where this guy was and probably thousands of people all over the place. So, we decided to go to the second floor and see if there was a gate there. When we got off the elevator, the only thing that was there were the bathrooms. Now, we were even more lost. Norma decided to take the steps to see if there was another gate. Coming up the steps at the end of a very long corridor was a gentleman who was coming up the steps on his way to the men's room with a sign under his arm that read, 'Don & Norma Honig'. With that, Norma said, 'that's us'.

Talk about intervention. Did we give God the credit that was His? No, we were too busy getting all our bags and waiting for this guy to take us to our location.

The second example took place just a few days ago when we were going to pick up some good friends at the Atlanta airport. To drive around the arrivals circuit takes about 15 minutes and we had driven the circuit about seven times hoping to see them come out of the baggage claim area because you could not wait, with the Atlanta police moving any and all waiting cars. Anyway, as we started to drive around for the eighth time, Norma suggested we park at the very end of the waiting area, which was a good 15 minute walk from the baggage claim area where we thought they would be coming out of. As we started to wait, we heard a bang on the window only to see it was our friends who decided to come up the wrong steps at the wrong end of the arrival lane and a 30-second walk to the car.

God once again had intervened and kept us from having to drive around this 15 minute arrival circuit again. Again, thank you Lord.

I said all that to say this, how many times has God intervened in our lives and chose to remain anonymous, which means according to Dictionary.com., without any name acknowledged, just like what we saw in the book of Esther. God is not mentioned by name, but His presence is all over the book as His presence is all over our lives.

More than once God has stepped in to the pages of our lives and saved us, bailed us out, delivered us, helped us out of a sticky situation. We hear an unspoken voice say walk this way, go that way, do this or do that. It's not a gut-feeling or a hunch or a coincidence. It was God, who had intervened on our behalf for the sake of His own reputation.

Let's give God the credit that belongs to Him. I believe many of us are alive today because God has intervened on our behalf and kept us from harm's way or death's door.

Do we actually see God doing that in scripture? You bet. How about in Daniel chapter 6, where Daniel is thrown in to the lion's den? Who shut the mouths of the lions? Or how about in the same book in chapter 4, verse 25, where it says; "But I see four men, untied and walking around in the midst of the fire! No harm has come to them! And the appearance of the fourth is like that of a god." And what about in **Acts 12:7,** suddenly an angel of the Lord appeared, and a light shone in the prison cell. He struck Peter on the side and woke him up, saying, "Get up quickly!" And the chains fell off Peter's wrists. And what about verse 10, when they were walking past the first and second guards and an iron locked gate opened for them by itself.

And how about in our own lives when an Angel of the Lord delivered us or our family or saved us from a car accident or from slipping on the ice or reminded us that the oven was still on at home or told us to call a friend who was sick and needed a word of comfort or maybe we got a call from a friend with a word from the Lord and it was exactly what we needed to confirm what we have been asking for.

Let's give credit where the credit is due

Thank you Lord for your intimacy in our lives and the lives of our families and friends, even when we are not aware of your presence.

Prayer: Lord, help me to give you all the credit for the things You are doing in my life and not to take any credit for anything because all things come from You.

1. Do you consider taking credit for something that is not yours a form of stealing? How do you think the Lord feels when we take credit for something that He did in our lives?
2. Do you believe the expression; 'All we can do well without God is fail' has any bearing on giving credit where credit is due? Regardless if you answered yes or no, why do you feel that way?

WEEK 8
The Heart That Cares

It's absolutely amazing how God can speak to us in any situation using anything that He wants to get His message across and His messages can really change your life forever.

A number of weeks ago, Norma and I were staying with some dear friends in Georgia; something happened that I really would like to share with you.

These friends subscribe to a medical journal and as I was walking in the kitchen, the Lord spoke to me as only He can speak and said, "Look at the magazine on the table." So being the obedient person that I am, at least in this one case, I glanced down to see the title of the main article which read; looking for the Heart that Cares. Obviously, it had something to do with a cardiovascular issue, but the title jumped off the magazine and spoke to my Spirit. Thank you Lord.

I began to think about society in general and many of my friends and the hurts and needs that exist in our world and in their lives.

I realized that people are looking for a heart that cares. I think you'll agree that people need to know they matter and that there's someone out there that unconditionally loves them in spite of their faults. You know what I mean, someone that we can be real not ideal or plastic with. Someone that we don't have to do a favor to get attention or acceptance in return. In other words, someone who loves us for who we are, not what we can do or what they get from us.

Sometimes, it seems that everyone wants a piece of the action. The government, the IRS, school, teachers, friends, family and the list just goes on and on. No wonder at the end of the day, we are so exhausted and it's not just from work. There are pressures without and pressures within that all have a tendency to work on our emotional state and wear us down.

Often times, we just get tired of performing for others, regardless of who they are. That's probably why we look forward to the weekend or a vacation or just being alone, and when I say alone, I mean alone without our mind beating us up or reminding us of what we so desperately need to forget. That's why sometimes, we yell and tell others; I need some rest.

You know in **Psalms 4:1**, David says exactly the same thing when he said; Answer me when I call to you, O God who declares me innocent. Free me from my troubles. Have mercy on me and hear my prayer. In other words, give me relief from my distress, I need some rest.

Well, I have great news, there is a place of rest and there is someone that loves us unconditionally and there is a heart that cares so much that He provides us with the very thing that we so desperately need.

I know you know the scripture, but you and I need to know that we really know who this person is and where that rest is. Head knowledge really doesn't seem to cut it when we are confronted with life size issues and troubles.

I know my medication will help me, but if I don't use it, what's the point in knowing that it will help me? Knowing there's a place of rest doesn't help me unless I go there to rest. Knowing that someone loves me unconditionally doesn't do me any good if I continue to act and perform to get His acceptance and love. That's not rest, that's work.

Jesus tells us in **Matthew 11:28**, Come to me, all who are tired from carrying heavy loads, and I will give you rest. One thing I know is that a person can't give what they don't have, yet here, Jesus says He will give us rest.

In **Hebrews 4:1,** it tells us; "God's promise is that we may enter his place of rest still stands." And in **Hebrews 4:9,** it takes it a step further and says "Therefore, a time of rest and worship exists for God's people."

That's pretty comforting to know that:

1. Jesus gives us that rest
2. His promise for that rest still stands, and
3. That rest period really does exist.

I guess the problem with rest is in the definition that we give to rest.

Bing says rest is: 1. Cessation of work, exertion, or activity. 2. Peace, ease, or refreshment resulting from sleep or the cessation of an activity.

In Greek, rest is to be exempt or to have an intermission.

We sometimes define rest as a few minutes break in a fast paced, hectic race through the day.

A Washington newspaper carried the story of Tattoo the basset hound a while back. Tattoo didn't intend to go for an evening run, but when his owner shut the dog's leash in the car door and took off for a drive – with Tattoo still outside the vehicle, he had no choice. Motorcycle officer, Terry Filbert noticed a passing vehicle with something dragging behind it. He commented that the poor basset hound was, "picking them up and putting them down as fast as he could." He chased the car to a stop, and Tattoo was rescued. But not before the dog had reached a top speed of 25 miles per hour, falling down and rolling over several times.

You know, too many of us are living our lives like Tattoo, picking them up and putting them down as fast as we can – rolling around & feeling dragged through life.

We need a time out from the rat race, and so, I have good news for you.

Jesus gives us rest, his promise for that, rest still stands, and that rest period really does exist. Let's take advantage of it and take time to smell the roses.

Prayer: Lord, you told me in your word that you have given me rest, help me to walk in the rest that belongs to me.

1. If the Lord gives us rest, but we are not walking in it, does that mean someone or something has stolen it? Think about your answer.
2. If you're not walking in rest, do you believe that God really gave it to you?

3. The Word tells us that there is a resting place for the children of God. Where do you think that resting place is? Is it spiritual or physical or both?
4. Is there a relationship between the resting place of God and the peace of God? Why?

Week 9
Illusions

The other day I was watching a program on Netflix that had to do with the best illusionists in the world, and as I was watching them perform their illusions, I was amazed at how they could make you believe something that looked so real, and yet, you knew it was untrue.

To make an elephant disappear from behind a curtain is just untrue or to make an actual jet materialize from behind a cardboard box is just imaginary, regardless of how real it looks.

What is an illusionist, or as some dictionaries say, a magician or conjurer or image maker. Whatever name you give them, they are really just a show business person there to perform their tricks as a form of entertainment. Don't get me wrong, what they do really is entertaining, and will amaze your senses regardless of how hard you look to see if you can find a fault in their trick or anything that will give away their secret.

What really is an illusion? Some other words for illusion are: dream or fantasy or mirage and some others define it as pipe dream or flight of fancy or even a daydream. In other words, it's not reality or fact; it's all make-believe, just to entertain the audience.

Here's the bottom line, an illusion is a lie and its purpose is to make a lie seem real and fool you into thinking what you saw or heard is the real thing.

Many of us may not know any professional illusionist personally, but the sad truth is we deal with a real illusionist every day of our life. We are daily confronted with a professional liar whose sole purpose is to get us to believe something that is not true. Not only are we dealing with a professional liar, but this illusionist can do nothing, but speak lies about us.

Sometimes, we might be entertained by lies, but we are told Lying lips are an abomination to the Lord, but those who act faithfully are his delight, **Proverbs 12:22**. It's bad enough that we have to listen to this professional liar, but he's also a murderer and the Word tells us: He was a murderer from the beginning, and has nothing to do with the truth, because there is no truth in him. When he lies, he speaks out of his own character, for he is a liar and the father of lies **John 8:44**. Just a thought, sometimes, I wonder if it means that the enemy murders the truth in believers.

How many times have we heard, never give away the secret of a trick? This especially applies to illusionists or magicians that perform their tricks. Why is that? Well for one, if everyone knew how an illusionists performs his illusions, it wouldn't be entertaining anymore and whatever they do wouldn't be great, just nice, but you would already know how they do it, so the thrill wouldn't be there.

I can remember watching someone do a card trick that I do all the time. Every move and shuffle this guy did with the cards, I already knew what was coming next and what the outcome would be. Was the trick exciting to me? No, of course not, because I already knew the truth and the outcome.

The illusionist that we deal with all the time is called the enemy or Satan. He is almost constantly trying to pull the wool over our eyes and trick us into believing something that is a lie. One lie that is obvious is when Satan disguises himself as an angel of light, **2 Corinthians 11:14**. We also know from The One who cannot lie that the great dragon was thrown down, that ancient serpent, who is called the devil and Satan, the deceiver of the whole world, **Revelation 12:9**. What exactly is a deceiver? It's someone that's a fraud, liar and cheat. But even more important, it's someone that's trying to get you to believe something that is not true.

There's a time for receiving and there's a time for refusing. When God is speaking, it's a time to receive because it will either strengthen, edify, encourage, and give you hope. When the enemy speaks, it's time to refuse, or make void and null because those words will only destroy, weaken, tear down and bring despair. We know these words as the works of the devil, but praise be to God because we are told in **John 3:8b** "That the reason that the Son of God appeared or was manifested was to destroy what the devil does or the works of the devil." Let me say this, to destroy something means to terminate, finish and put an end to. So, we are told the truth, which is that Jesus Christ was manifested or revealed to finish and put an end to everything the enemy does and says, which includes his false illusions, lies and cheap shots about the children of the Living God.

Is that good news? Sure it is, because it means the master illusionist's tricks and deceptions have been revealed and carry absolutely no weight because we know they're not true. Not only that, but we are not to fall for his tricks and lies and we can and must put on the whole armor of God, that we may be able to stand against the schemes of the devil, **Ephesians 6:11**. You can cut the enemy off even before he starts his lies concerning you, after all, we are told, and give no opportunity to the devil **Ephesians 4:7**. That means don't even entertain his conversation, not even for a second.

How do I do that? Choose which voice you want to listen to. God says you can, the enemy says you can't. God says you are, the enemy says you are not. God says you have, the enemy says you have not. Whose report will you believe? We don't have to be fooled by the enemy's words, we must come to that place that we will not be outwitted by Satan; for we are not ignorant of his designs, **2 Corinthians 2:11**.

Is it easy? Of course not, but remember we do not wrestle against flesh and blood, but against the rulers, against the authorities, against the cosmic powers over this present darkness, against the spiritual forces of evil in the heavenly places, **Ephesians 6:12**.

We can have victory over the enemy because we have been told: submit yourselves therefore to God. Resist the devil, and he will flee from you, **James 4:7**. We also know that the Lord your God is he who goes with you to fight for you against your enemies, to give you the victory, **Deuteronomy 20:4**.

My friends, not only do we have victory over the enemy, but it also has been given to you authority to tread on serpents and scorpions, and over all the power of the enemy, and nothing shall hurt you.

Prayer: Father, I know in my head that you do all things decently and in order and you never speak in double meanings, also, you have the best intentions for my life. Help me to internalize this truth so I can discern between your truth and what the enemy tries to tell me.

1. Do you sometimes get so confused that you don't know if the conversation is from God, yourself or the enemy?
2. If we know the enemy is a liar and the father of lies, why do we entertain his conversation?
3. Have you ever believed something was of God only to find out it was not? How did you feel and what did you do about it?

WEEK 10
How God Speaks Through a Grape Seed

The other day at the breakfast table, we were all having coffee, fruit and cheese, a typical Israeli breakfast. As I was eating some grapes, and my method is, I crush the seeds with the grape and eat them both. I know some like to remove the seeds first, but since there are no hard copy rules for grapes, I crush them and usually don't pay any attention to them.

Anyway, I put this one grape in my mouth, and for some reason, I was inclined to remove a large seed and look at it. At that very moment, the Lord spoke to me about seeds and the law of seeds. I don't know if there really is something called a law of seeds, but for me, now, it's a law of seeds.

I removed this one seed and began to stare at it. The Lord showed me that if this one seed was properly cared for, it could feed every person on the face of the earth. This seed could reproduce and create other plants like itself, and with enough plants, there would be a vineyard each having millions of other grapes with millions and millions of seeds each capable of reproducing itself. I just sat there staring and amazed with what the Lord was downloading for me.

As a biologist, I know a seed is the part of a plant which can grow into a new plant, with a reproductive structure which disperses, and can survive for some time. I know that. And it doesn't matter if it's a grape seed or an apple seed or an orange seed. One seed can make a difference to the entire world if properly taken care of with right temperatures, water, sunlight and you know the rest.

I said thank you Lord for showing this to me. He responded by saying; "Here's where the teaching starts, not ends". And what a teaching it was. You see, I know the Seed of God is the Word of God. I also know it is the Seed of God's Words that produces the spiritual fruit in our spirits. **Luke 8:11** which tells us: "This is what the story illustrates: The seed is God's word.

The question the Lord asked me and now I ask you is: "If a natural seed is that part of a plant which can grow into a new plant, with a reproductive structure which disperses, and can survive for some time, is the seed of God capable of doing the same thing? Can the seed of God grow into a new plant or believer with the ability to also reproduce, disperse and survive for some time"? To re-phrase the question, can the Word of God which we agree with be the seed of God; can it make such an impact on a person's life that it will completely change them into a new creation? Can this new creation be able to reproduce and survive for a long time?

Luke 13:19 tells us: It's like a mustard seed that someone planted in a garden. It grew and became a tree, and the birds nested in its branches." We all know why birds nest in a tree. It's a place of security, comfort, a place to raise their young, a place for feeding the young and a place to sleep in the evening. So! Is the Word of God a place of security, a place of comfort and a place for feeding the young believers? You bet it is.

Does the seed or God's word need to be cared for and protected? Well, according to **Luke 8: 5-11**, which tells us: "A farmer went to plant his seeds. Some seeds were

43

planted along the road, were trampled, and were devoured by birds. Others were planted on rocky soil. When the plants came up, they withered because they had no moisture. Others were planted among thorn bushes. The thorn bushes grew up with them and choked them. Others were planted on good ground. When they came up, they produced a hundred times as much as was planted." After he had said this, he called out, "Let the person who has ears listen!"

One other thing about seeds is that they are very delicate and easily destroyed, and therefore, need to be protected as we can see in the verses we just read. The word of God is the same thing. It is not to be treated lightly, discarded, ignored, wasted or allowed to be choked out by the things of the world. Why? You might be asking? Because the fruit is nothing like the original seed. An apple seed or grape seed or orange seed doesn't look anything like the apple, grape or orange. This is confirmed in **1Corinthians 15:37**; what you plant, whether its wheat or something else, is only a seed. It doesn't have the form that the plant will have.

The word of God planted in you will change you and you will be completely different than what you started out as. To that, I say thank God. And not only that, the new you can be a reproductive structure which disperses, and can survive. Oh, by the way, this is also confirmed in **1John 3:9,** "Everyone who has been born of God does not commit sin, because His seed remains in him, and he cannot sin, because he has been born of God."

That sounds like a new you and a new me which is completely different from when we first started out. When I look back over where I came from, I am always so thankful for the Word of God or seed which has changed my life. The new me doesn't look anything like the old me, to which you should be thankful.

Prayer: Father, help me to water the seed that you have planted in my life and not allow it to die because of bad soil, lack of water or the cares of the world.

1. Do you believe the seed that God has planted in your spirit has the ability to grow and reproduce?
2. What things in your life have a tendency to kill the seed of God in you or your spirit?

WEEK 11
Life Is Like a Roller Coaster Ride

The other day, I was reminiscing over the lifestyle the Lord has allowed us to participate in over the past five years and it brings to mind the scripture found in **Proverbs 16:9**, we can make our plans, but the LORD determines our steps.

In other words and to paraphrase this verse, you have no idea where the first step of your journey is going to take you. You may have an idea what you want or what you would like, but it's just an idea because God directs our footsteps.

Sometimes, I joke and say that Norma and I are like Jewish Bedouins traveling the world and doing the Lord's work. Sometimes, people ask us 'where do we live' and my response is 'where am I now'? The only things we own are locked up in storage and getting less every year, as we determine that we really don't need them. We are joyfully downsizing in a world that seems to think that upsizing is the way to go.

The Lord has re-defined my understanding of security. I use to think that security meant having "things" and a place to put them. It almost reminds me of my favorite quote, which is found in the movie, Crocodile Dundee where he says, "It's like two fleas arguing over who owns the dog." In other words, who you are, what you own and where you live is not your own. We are children of the Most High first and stewards of His possessions second.

Job had it right in **Job 1:21**; He said, "Naked I came from my mother, and naked I will return. The LORD has given, and the LORD has taken away! May the name of the LORD be praised."

But now, I realize that I am not in control of my life and when I try to be in control, I find that I become part of the problem and not the solution. But when God is in control, a great weight is taken from my shoulders. How you might ask? By believing in **Proverbs 3:6** which tell us; Seek his will in all you do, and he will show you which path to take.

Is this a good rule to follow? You bet because **Isaiah 46:10** says only I can tell you the future before it even happens. Everything I plan will come to pass, for I do whatever I wish.

If God is as good as He says He is and as loving as we know He is, then truth be told, He will direct our foot steps in to areas of blessings. He wouldn't ask us to do something that would not be to His liking and intentionally try to destroy us or bring us to ruin. Does **Jeremiah 29:11** sound like a plan for destruction? It tells us; for I know the plans I have for you," says the LORD. "They are plans for good and not for disaster, to give you a future and a hope. The problem is He knows the plans He has for us and He may or may not share those plans with us. In other words, we would really like to know the plans that He has for us before those plans happen and if we don't like those plans, we want to go for plan B immediately.

You might say to yourself, I have a great idea; I think I'll do this and go there. It might be a great idea according to you, but since you were bought for a price and no longer belong to yourself, the Lord will determine your steps.

Truth be told, if you are sold out for Him, and you don't like where He's directing you, bite the bullet because **Jeremiah 10:23** tells us; "I know, O LORD, that a man's life is not his own; it is not for man to direct his steps." In addition, **Psalm 37:23** tells us; "If the LORD delights in a man's way, he makes his steps firm."

When does the Lord delight in a man's way? When the man is doing the Lord's will. If we are not doing the Lord's will, how can we expect Him to delight in what we are doing?

It's like the verse that says, "The joy of the Lord is my strength." Well, what exactly is the joy of the Lord or what brings the Lord joy? It's obvious that the Lord is joyful when His children are obedient and walking in His ways.

If you are like me, and say I don't understand what you are doing Lord, He will respond by saying "I know that", that's why **Proverbs 20:24** confirms this by telling us; a man's steps are directed by the LORD. How then can anyone understand his own way?

Nowhere in scripture do I find where we have to know and understand what God is doing in our lives before we will do what He wants us to do. I guess that's where the 'trust' issue comes into play. I don't have to know what you are doing in my life in order for me to trust you; I just have to know you. This is why **Psalm 91:2** tells us; this I declare about the LORD: He alone is my refuge, my place of safety; he is my God, and I trust him, and again in **Psalm**

37:5; "Commit everything you do to the LORD. Trust him, and he will help you."

Nowhere does it say we first have to know everything about Him. So a life committed to the Lord is a walk of trust. Did you notice I said a life committed to the Lord and not a life as a world traveler or a missionary to the furthest parts of the globe or a stand on a box on the corner and preach the word? If you are a house wife committed to the Lord, your life will reflect it, if you are a businessman, your life will reflect it, if you are a student, your life will reflect it. No matter what you do, if your life is a committed life to the Lord, it will reflect the characteristics of the Lord to everyone around you. It will also be a life of trust since you do not know the ending from the beginning. As a matter of fact, you don't even know what the next 10 minutes will bring.

There's a reason why when you first get on a roller coaster they ask you to buckle up and grab a strong hold of the hand rail. At that very moment, there's really no need for a hand rail or when you start the climb to the top of the ride, there's still no reason for the hand rail, but when you take that first steep sharp drop, thank God for the buckle and the hand rail.

My friends, life is like a roller coaster ride, we buckle up, grab the hand rail and put our trust in God, He will bring us through because God and only God is faithful.

Prayer: Heavenly Father, help me to walk in and understand that my life is in your hands and you are directing the steps of my life.

1. If your life is like a roller coaster ride, what defines the ups and downs of your hectic life?
2. If you don't understand what God is doing in your life, can you still trust Him with your life?

WEEK 12
Never Give Up

The other day, I received really good news from a friend of mine in Israel concerning a mutual friend of ours who also lives in Israel and who has been fasting for three weeks for God to respond with an answer to a critical situation. Well, God did respond with an 11:59 miracle and we were truly joyful. Not only did God respond, but with an exceedingly abundantly response.

Have you ever noticed how easy it is to look back over our shoulder to see the miracle in our lives that God has provided for us and the joy we experience when the need has been provided for? It's a lot different from the experience we are in while the waiting process is all around us. It's like being in a dark tunnel and not being able to see the light at the end of the tunnel.

As I'm fond of saying, I don't like being in a tunnel, I don't see why I have to be in a tunnel and I can think of 20 people more deserving to be here in this tunnel than me. Bottom line, Tunnel 101 is not for me, neither is tunnel 102 or 110 or 250. The only thing that often times keep us going is the fact that God is faithful in the midst of every tunnel in life. After all, didn't He say He would never leave us nor forsake us? That means in the tunnels, as-well-as the mountain top experiences. Truth is, in the tunnels we ask for help, on the mountain tops, we give Him thanks.

In the musical Les Miserable which just came out, there's a statement in the play which is so very true. It says, 'that which is coming has not yet arrived'. Doesn't that sounds like a waiting process for a prayer that is really important to us?

I said all that to say this, there's a movie called Galaxy Quest, which is a science fiction comedy, but there's a re-occurring statement in the movie that came to my remembrance as my friend in Israel was in this dark tunnel period of his life. It was the statement: 'Never give up'. You know, when you don't see the answer to the problem and the time is getting close to where a decision has to be made, it's easy to think of giving up as a solution. But the movie and the Lord reassure us; never give up, never.

It brings to mind a picture of an old water pump with the rusty old handle; you know the type, the old fashion hand pump that you need to keep on pumping until the fresh, clear, cold water begins to flow from the nozzle. Sometimes, the water has to travel a really long distance because the water bed is down a long way. You keep on pumping, and after 5 minutes, you decide to give up because maybe the pump is broken or the well is dry or for whatever excuse we can think of. Truth be told, the water actually traveled all the way up the pipe until it was just five pumps away, but we got tired, made excuses and gave up. The water fell back to the deep water bed far below the surface because we didn't hang in there, and yet, it was so close, but we couldn't see it. I guess that's called living by sight and not by faith.

Is there a benefit in hanging in there? Daniel thought so in **Daniel 10:12** where it tells us: "He told me, 'don't be afraid, Daniel. God has heard everything that you said ever since the first day you decided to humble yourself in front of your God so that you could learn to understand things. I have come in response to your prayer.' "

Listen to this next verse in **Daniel 9:23,** As soon as you began to pray, an answer was given, which I have come to tell you, for you are highly esteemed'.

You know, Daniel could have thought God is busy or there's something wrong and my prayers won't get answered, so I may as well just give up. But Daniel knew that God is faithful to answer. You see, Daniel knew that in **Isaiah 65:24,** it tells him and it tells us; 'Before they call I will answer; while they are still speaking I will hear'. That means never give up.

Why did Daniel's prayers, and often times, our own prayers get held up or not answered when we want them answered? I mean how come we don't get the response immediately, after all, it's really important to me. The answer to that question can be found in **Daniel 10:13** where it tells us: 'But for twenty-one days, the spirit prince of the kingdom of Persia blocked my way. Then Michael, one of the archangels, came to help me, and I left him there with the spirit prince of the kingdom of Persia.'

The enemy doesn't want our prayers to be answered and giving up is not of God, but the enemy. Often times, our prayers get held up in a spiritual battle which we are not aware of, but the truth is; what, then, shall we say in response to this? If God is for us, who can be against us as it tells us in **Romans 8:31**. That, my friend, is a never give up statement.

If you are waiting for an answer to a prayer that you lifted up to God, don't stop and never give up, never give up. That which is coming has not yet arrived, but it is on the way.

Prayer: Lord, sometimes when I find myself in a tunnel of life, help me to still trust in you, although, I can't see any light at the end of the tunnel.

1. When you find yourself in a place not of your choosing and you don't see any way out, can you still trust that God is there with you?
2. Deep down in this hectic life you experience, do you really believe that God is in control of your out of controls? If so, have you given Him all control or are you trying to help God in the details?

WEEK 13
Not a Moment in Time But a Journey for Life

You know, the other day while I was mediating on nothing specific, but everything in general, an inner voice spoke to me and said "increase your vision."

I've read something kind of similar in **Isaiah 54:2,** where it says to; "Expand the space of your tent. Stretch out the curtains of your tent, and don't hold back. Lengthen your tent ropes, and drive in the tent pegs."

Next, I heard the Lord say, do you know what this means to you to increase your vision? To which I responded; "Yes, of course, I know what this means to me." After 30 years of walking with the Lord, you would have thought that I knew when the Lord asks me a question; the obvious is not the obvious and He was looking for a revolution in my thinking.

I responded that to expand the space of my tent or expand my vision was to make the building or the ministry or the works, or the teaching and preaching bigger and to drive in the tent pegs was to secure the expansion.

I'm so grateful that God speaks to me in a way where there is no confusion. He said "Wrong". That's all He said, wrong! Well, there's no way of confusing 'wrong'. It means you are not right. God does as He pleases and says what He wants.

So like Job, I stood up and asked; "Why is it wrong"? To which He said, "I asked what it means to you, not to my Body".

I was thinking like so many, let's increase the size of the buildings or let's expand the size of the ministry. Let's get more seats and fit more people into the service, let's get a few more buses for the Sunday service, let's get a radio or television program, so more people can hear us. Don't misunderstand me, there's nothing wrong with that if the Lord told you to do it, but unfortunately many ministries fold up because they thought that's what the Lord said and it wasn't Him at all.

I guess it's true that there is wisdom in the counsel of the wise. At least when you get together with Godly men and women on a decision that's important to you, it's a lot wiser than you making the decision based on what you think or feel. I once heard it said that a person all wrapped up in himself makes a very small package.

Praise the Lord that we serve a speaking God, not like what we find in **Habakkuk 2: 18-20**. "What benefit is there in a carved idol when its maker has carved it? What benefit is there in a molded statue, a teacher of lies, when its maker has molded it? The one who formed it trusts himself to make worthless idols that cannot speak. How horrible it will be for the one who says to a piece of wood, "Wake up!" and to a stone that cannot talk, "Get up!"' Can that thing teach anyone? Just look at it! It's covered with gold and silver, but there's absolutely no life in it." The LORD is in his holy temple. All the earth should be silent in his presence.

So I said "Lord, I thought I knew what increase your vision means to me, but I was wrong."

He responded and said, "To you, it means enlarge your vision of who I am. To expand the space of your tent is to have a greater understanding of the Lord your God and know that with Me, nothing is impossible. Don't put me in a box when the heavens themselves cannot hold me."

Soooo, as I thought on this, I realized once again that God was right and the vision that I had of Him was way too small. I mean I know that God is big, but that's just a word that I use to explain something that I cannot understand. Really, who can understand just how big God is?

So my next question was simple, how do I go about expanding my vision of just how big my God is? It's not like I can go to a book store and pick up How to increase your understanding of how big God is in three simple steps.

God said, "This is not a moment in time, but a journey of life." I understand that to mean, the more time I spend with Him, the more I get to know Him, the more I recognize His voice, the more I trust Him. Truly, that is not a moment in time, but a journey of life that I'm ready to take. Knowing Him is what it's all about because it's always been about Him, is all about Him and will be about Him.

Prayer: God, help me to increase in my understanding of who you are in my journey through life and help me to be part of the solution and not the problem.

1. Do you believe that God is more interested in your destination or your journey in life?
2. Where do you believe intimacy with God comes from, the destination or the long drawn out journey? Justify your answer using scripture.

Week 14
But Lord, I Don't Want to be Here

Today's message is not only extremely necessary, but extremely needed and deals with a topic that many, if not all of us have been through at some point in our walk and some are probably there right now. Does the expression 'but Lord, I don't want to be here' ring a bell?

Sure it does, every time we find ourselves in a wilderness experience, Lord, I don't want to be here. When we find ourselves surrounded by winds and waves, Lord I don't want to be here, or when we open our eyes and find we are in a lion's den, Lord, I don't want to be here or how about in a fiery furnace, Lord, I don't want to be here. Let's take it a little closer to home, when the doctors tell you there's no hope, Lord, I don't want to be here or you get a call in the middle of the night from the police station that your child has been arrested, Lord, I don't want to be here or maybe your underage son or daughter tells you, Mom, you're going to be a grandmother, Lord, I don't want to be here. You know there are so many scenarios that can be used where the response is Lord, I don't want to be here. What are we actually saying? Lord, this is not what I signed up for when I said yes to You. I know you didn't promise me a rose garden, but this large patch of thorns covering my life isn't exactly what I had in mind either.

Losing one's spouse or finding ourselves in a situation like many in the Philippians after the most powerful storm ever to be recorded has just left you with nothing, no home, water, food, family, nothing not even a slim hope that there might be something left is a 'Lord, I don't want to be here' situation. Unfortunately, the truth is, although you don't want to be there, that's where you are and it will probably take some time until that fact becomes a reality. When you wake up from this nightmare, you realize you weren't sleeping and the question becomes what do I do now or where do I go from here?

Personally, when I find myself in one of those 'Lord, I don't want to be here' situations, and I've been in quite a few of them, I find that if I can't get out of the situation, the next best thing is to invite the Lord in to the situation. His presence is more than just a comforting word on paper; it's a comforting reality to a life that's pretty shaken up.

How many times have we honestly looked at our life and wish we could have traded it with someone else thinking their life is a piece of cake. Or we think to ourselves how did I ever end up in this situation; it has to be a mistake. And yet, we are told in **Psalms 27:23** the steps of a good man are ordered or directed or managed by the LORD: and he takes pleasure in his way. Again in **1 Samuel 2:9,** we are told He will guard the feet of his faithful servants, but the wicked will be silenced in the place of darkness. It is not by strength that one prevails.

What does this mean? It means that where we find ourselves is not a mistake, we are not here by accident, although we wish we could blame where we are on anything or anyone, but God knew well in advance that this day in our life was not only quickly coming upon us, but was actually ordered and directed by the Lord himself.

And I'm sure that God doesn't expect us to come to this conclusion immediately and be able to cast this life shaking event behind us in the blinking of an eye. Healing sometimes takes time and this is why we are told that God guards the feet of his faithful servants. This is why we are told in **Psalm 40:2,** He lifted me out of the slimy pit, out of the mud and mire; he set my feet on a rock and gave me a firm place to stand.

When we find ourselves smack in the middle of a disaster in life, it really seems like we are stuck in a slimy pit or held fast in mud that won't let us go; we feel like we are sinking in quicksand with no way out because our thinking is consumed by the issue that has shaken our lives.

I've learned a secret which is very true, in quicksand, the thing that draws you down to your doom is not the sand, but the movement within the sand. Authorities tell us to avoid being consumed by the sand, the trick is to lay back and do absolutely nothing, don't move. Almost like **Psalm 46:10**; "Cease striving and know that I am God. Cease striving means stop all activity."

God is such a good God that once we are able to stand on our own two feet, the next thing that God does for us is explained in **Psalm 18:19.** He brought me out into a spacious place; he rescued me because he delighted in me.

So we have gone from a patch of quick sand or mud/mire or swamp where we can't move to a spacious field where we can run with no end in sight and know that He goes before our running in a freedom the likes of which we think we had lost forever.

You know, personally when I have found myself in a situation in life that is so far out of my control and seemingly the darkness is closing in on me, the first thing that goes is my ability to use my Christ centered reasoning. The problem becomes much larger than God's promises and I begin to despair and wonder if that's how it's going to be. At this point, like Peter, the only prayer I can force out is Lord, help. I don't have the strength to put together a prayer that is grammatically and spiritually correct. All I can say is 'help' and you know what? That's enough to cause God to respond and when He shows up, things happen as we're told in **Romans 15:13,** "But the God of hope shall fill you with all joy and peace by faith, that you shall super abound in his hope by the power of The Spirit of Holiness."

My friend, if you are in that shadow of no hope or find yourselves entering into that place in life that you would rather not be in, trust in God and know this, it will not be forever, He has never left you nor abandoned you and you won't be there forever. If you can't get out of that place, I encourage you to invite God into that place; He is faithful to take you by the hand and lead you out to a spacious place filled with His presence.

Prayer: Father, I know when I acknowledge you in all my ways, you direct my footsteps. Help me not to complain and murmur when those footsteps take me to places that would not be of my first choice.

1. How to you act when you find yourself in a situation that you don't want to be in, although you believe it's from the Lord? Why do you act that way?
2. Is it difficult for you to step outside of your comfort zone, especially if something that you are doing is for the Lord?
3. If God sent you, do you believe that God will also take care of you where he sends you?

WEEK 15
Safety, Security and a Deliverer

A few months ago when I was in Atlanta GA walking in the backyard by the pool, I thought my eyes were playing tricks on me because out of the corner of my eye I noticed something small and black swimming in the pool. I turned to watch this tiny creature as it swan back and forth from the shallow end to the deep end and back again.

Obviously, this tiny shrew had inadvertently fallen into the water and was trying desperately to get out of the water which if not delivered would become its watery grave.

As I watched, this tiny animal would swim by the ladder, completely ignoring it's only means of safety. The ladder was a place of safety, but not deliverance.

All of a sudden during one of its laps in the pool, the shrew discovered the ladder and made for the nearest rung on the ladder. It climbed out of the pool and shook the water off its body. It was now safe, but its place of safety was 18 inches long and 3 inches wide and no place to go. If it went down, it was back in the water and the nearest other rung was way out of its reach.

As I sat there looking at this helpless creature, I began to mediate on how many times I've been in a similar situation and realized that a place of safety is not the answer.

This little animal walked the length of the rung about six times and realized that his walking back and forth was not the answer, it needed something else. All of a sudden, it stopped and just sat there for the longest time.

63

I'm going to take the liberty and say that it realized that it needed a deliverer. I'm taking that liberty because many times I just had to stop and realize that I needed a deliverer and all my actions and travels were not going to get me out the place of safety which would become my grave.

It brought to my remembrance something I was very fond of saying; 'the difference between a rut and a grave is how long you stay there'. In other words, a place of safety will eventually become your grave if your surroundings are not changed. What is needed is a deliverer.

I decided that I was going to be the deliverer of this shrew and set him free. As I approached the animal, it began to get really agitated and visibly fearful. For a moment, I thought it would jump back into the water.

I knew if I reached down to lift it up, it was for sure going to bite me. I thought to myself' 'give me a break, I'm here to save you and you want to bite me'. You have no reason to be fearful.

I heard of a situation like that before in **Matthew 14: 25-27**. Between three and six o'clock in the morning, Jesus came to them. He was walking on the sea. When the disciples saw him walking on the sea, they were terrified. They said, "It's a ghost!" and began to scream because they were afraid. Immediately, Jesus said, "Calm down! It's me. Don't be afraid!" I would have said, give me a break, I'm here to deliver you and you want to bite me out of fear.

I'm sure I could have said calm down! It's me. Don't be afraid! But that would have been a waste of time because this helpless little animal wouldn't understand me. Very similar to the many times the Lord has said to me, Calm down! It's me. Don't be afraid! And I didn't understand Him either. Like Peter, I had my eyes on the wind and the waves, not He who calms the wind and waves.

So I reached down and lifted the animal off the rung of the ladder with a stick and delivered him from his death.

What would you say if I told you that the next thing this creature did was to walk up to me and start licking my fingers and rubbed itself on my shoes and followed me all around the pool? It even let out a loud pitch sound and all its friends and family came out of the woods and formed a circle around me and sat down to thank this strange deliverer that just rescued one of its kind.

Well, it did just about what we all do, it took off as fast as it could into the woods, never even looking back at its hero, its deliverer, the one who saved him.

It made me think of **Psalms 46:1-3**. God is our place of safety. He gives us strength. He is always there to help us in times of trouble. The earth may fall apart. The mountains may fall into the middle of the sea. But we will not be afraid. The waters of the sea may roar and foam. The mountains may shake when the waters rise. But we will not be afraid.

This Psalm should help us to realize that we often times believe a lie when it comes to safety or security. Truth be told, we are no different from the Israelites in **Exodus 14:12**. Didn't we tell you to leave us alone while we were still in Egypt? Our Egyptian slavery was far better than dying out here in the wilderness!"

I'm going to take a guess and say this passage represents a failure in the school of faith. These people did not have faith in God.

We tell ourselves the lie that safety and security may be found in people. The Israelites thought there was more safety and security in serving the Egyptians than wandering in the desert. Many are also convinced that a President, politician or certain political party will bring better days and security to us.

It brings to memory the story of a little girl who once said to her mother, "Mommy, if Santa Claus brings our presents, and God gives us our daily bread, and Uncle Sam gives us Social Security, why do we keep daddy around?"

The question becomes what is the truth about safety and security?

Obedience to God is the ultimate security. In our **Exodus 14:12** text, the Israelites were willing to live as slaves in order to have food on the table. However, to live in Egypt was to disobey God. Moses knew that ultimate security depended upon obeying God and following His will for your life.

John Adams who was the second president of the United States and the son of John Adams Sr., a deacon in Congress, made a statement in 1755 according to SOURCE Prayer Team that stated; "It must be understood that there is no national security but in the nation's humble acknowledged dependence upon God and His overruling care and management." In other words, there is no national security, but to humbly acknowledge all dependency upon God and His power and His presence.

Jesus Himself understood this when He quoted **Psalm 31:5** "Into your hands I commit my spirit."

It was a prayer recognizing that God alone is our protector, our refuge, and our deliverer. It acknowledged that God was in control of suffering and anguish.

Let's face it; we all need a place to go to when we're stressed or sad, tired or lonely, fearful or tempted, disappointed or discouraged - a place where we can unload our burdens and get some relief.

Life is filled with problems, some small and some great, but the good news is there has been and will continue to be a source of strength, hope, promise and encouragement for each one of us. Let's all turn to and read together **Psalms 91,** which is an expression of the child of God's confidence in divine protection and deliverance.

Psalm 91: whoever goes to the Lord for safety, whoever remains under the protection of the Almighty, can say to him, "You are my defender and protector. You are my God; in you I trust." He will keep you safe from all hidden dangers and from all deadly diseases. He will cover you with his wings; you will be safe in his care; his faithfulness will protect and defend you. You need not fear any dangers at night or sudden attacks during the day or the plagues that strike in the dark or the evils that kill in daylight. A thousand may fall dead beside you, ten thousand all around you, but you will not be harmed. You will look and see how the wicked are punished. You have made the Lord your defender, the Most High your protector, and so no disaster will strike you, no violence will come near your home. God will put his angels in charge of you to protect you wherever you go. They will hold you up with their hands to keep you from hurting your feet on the stones. You will trample down lions and snakes, fierce lions and poisonous snakes. God says, "I will save those who love me and will protect those who acknowledge me as Lord. When they call to me, I will answer them; when they are in trouble, I will be with them. I will rescue them and honor them. I will reward them with long life; I will save them."

Prayer: Father, help me to realize the reason that Jesus is my savior and deliverer is because I have a need to be saved and delivered on a daily basis.

1. If Jesus is truly your savior and deliverer, what is He saving and delivering you from?
2. Do you think that as your savior and deliverer, Jesus needs your help in doing what He does best? If not, do you ever try to help the Lord in getting you out of a jam?

WEEK 16
Sometimes Life Seems Like a Grab Bag

You know I was thinking this morning how sometimes life seems like a grab bag. I know the steps of the righteous are ordered of the Lord and I know He directs our steps. But since I don't know the ending from the beginning, it sometimes seems that life is a grab bag.

I can just hear some of you now, what does he mean by a grab bag? Well, according to the American Heritage Dictionary of Idioms, a grab bag alludes to a container offered at a party or fair, where one gets a prize without knowing what one will get. You know what I mean, especially around Christmas, some stores will have a table filled with wrapped gifts and all for the same price, let's say $5.00. The only problem is you have no idea what's inside the package. You might get something worth $15.00 or something worth $1.00. Now, I'm not saying the Lord is going to short change us. What I am saying is that we have no idea what the future holds.

Give you an example; I woke up early this morning to the sounds of thunder. It was still dark outside and I was thinking to myself, is that really the sounds of thunder or rockets knowing that south of us 60 rockets were shelled into Israeli air space. Here in Israeli, we have come to live with a controlled expect the unexpected sort of way.

I began to think that, 15 years ago, working in the space shuttle program, life was pretty good and things would not change. Now, there's no space shuttle program. And I was saying to myself; 'who would have ever imagined that one day we would be living for a short time in Israel.' Although I can't speak for them, I'm pretty sure that my friends in Oman would be saying who would have ever imagined or our other friends in Jordan would be saying who would have ever imagined.

I'm sure there are dozens of you guys out there that have had major changes in your lives that you would have ever imagined. And you have come to realize as I have come to realize that life is like a roller coaster. One thing that I know about roller coasters when you first start the journey, they have hand rails to hold onto, but really, you don't need them because you're going really, really slow up-hill. After the first steep, sharp, fast drop you thank God for the hand rail and you look around to find your stomach that is somewhere right in your throat.

Let me give you an example, once when visiting Disney in Orlando; I decided to go on Space Mountain. Let me just say this up front, personally, I don't like fast rides. The escalator in the department store is about my speed. If I could, I'd put seat belts on my chair. I figured how bad it can really be. Bad enough it's in absolute darkness, but you would have thought the screams coming from the ride would have told me something. After my first sheer drop, the only thing in my mind was, 'who would have ever imagined'? Then, I repented for what came next.

I am so glad that He's in control of my out of controls. With God, there are no sheer drops or absolute darkness and no 'who would have ever imagined'. He doesn't pull the rug out from our feet to watch us stumble or fall. He is a firm foundation that we can build our lives upon and know that He is always there for us. When He says 'let's go to the other side', He means we will get to the other side regardless if a storm of life should come up out of nowhere. He is always bigger than the winds and waves and He still speaks to us and says, "It is I, don't be afraid".

Prayer: Father, I thank you that although often times I have no idea what's going on around me and life seems to be a shot in the dark, I am so thankful that you have me right in the palm of your hand and you carry me when I need divine assistance.

1. When life around you seems to be completely out of control, do you believe that God shares your feelings and opinions?
2. If God is completely in control of all the out of controls, why do you allow the circumstances to dictate how a child of the King will feel and think?

WEEK 17
Life Sometimes Seems Like a Heavy Overcast

I once learned that you can get major lessons from the Minor Prophets and you can also get big blessings from little teachings.

Today's sharing actually comes from a personal life experience that I went through when I first moved to Virginia Beach. We had left Florida and a well-paying job at the Space Center and moved North to Virginia. The thought sounded great on paper when I was in Florida, but the moment we hit Virginia, complete and almost what I thought was total despair set in and I didn't like anything about Virginia. I didn't have a job or a house or any friends or a congregation. I felt like God had abandoned me and I was in a deep state of leave me alone.

It was in the early morning in winter and really cold outside and I couldn't sleep. I grabbed a blanket and went outside to the cold stone porch and sat on the steps in the back yard. It was probably 2:30 in the morning. I remember speaking to the Lord and telling Him all my feelings, likes and dislikes and how I thought He had turned His back on me and I was left alone. I clearly remember looking up at the early morning sky and it was crystal clear and what seemed to be thousands of stars scattered all throughout the sky. I also clearly remembered there was not a single cloud in the sky. It was so clear that it surprised me. I glanced at the heavens and just stared into nothing. I turned away for probably 15 seconds because something caught my attention, but quickly turned back to looking at the stars. To my complete amazement, the stars were gone and very heavy, thick clouds filled the sky. As a matter-of-fact, there were so many clouds that not a single star was visible to the naked eye. It was just a very heavy over-cast.

At that very moment, the Lord spoke to me and asked the question "Are the stars still there?" I said what? He repeated the question, "Are the stars still there?" Of course, the stars are still there, I said. 'How can you be certain?' He asked. Because I know that I know. But you can't see them, He said, so how do you know they are there. Because the stars being present in the sky has nothing to do with the presence of the clouds. The stars are so much higher than the clouds.

I mean here I am all, wrapped up in a blanket, in the back yard at 2:30-ish on a freezing winter morning, speaking to God and being taught a lesson on stars and clouds, at least, that's what I thought. It was really something much deeper as I looked back over the meeting we had.

Next, God says, 'So although you cannot see the stars, you are absolutely convinced that they are present, is that what you are telling Me?' Yes, I boldly said. The next thing God said to me was; "Am I still here?" Yes, I said not so boldly. How do you know? You feel abandoned and alone, said God. I just know that you are here. Are you absolutely convinced that I am present in your life like the stars are present in the sky, asked God? Yes, I said. To which God said, that's good.

The whole conversation took about two minutes. Isn't it amazing how God can have a complete conversation and teach a heart touching lesson in the blinking of an eye.

The next thing I heard is, look up. And to my complete amazement, the sky was cloudless and the stars seemed larger and brighter, closer, and clearer. It was like I was in deep space, observing the heavens with all their stars. It actually took my breath away; they were so large and clear. You know, sometimes, we may have a very heavy overcast in our lives and we can't seem to make heads or tails out of life. We feel all alone and think no one can possibly understand what I am going through, not even God because He seems so far away.

The truth is He is just a prayer away and like the stars, although you may not feel or think He's present, He is very present and a very real fortress and tower in the midst of your life situation. We don't have to see Him to believe Him, we just have to believe Him. When He said I will never leave you or forsake you, He meant I will never abandon you or desert you or turn my back on you or leave you alone. What He said was I will stick closer to you than your shadow; I will be so close that every time you turn around, you will trip over my feet; I will be closer to you than a hug or an embrace. In other words, you may feel lonely, but you are never alone.

Prayer: Father, many times I feel like I'm all alone and its times like this that I need your manifested presence to shine through the darkness and be that light to my steps.

1. When the trials of life seem to be surrounding you and you don't see a way out, do you believe that God is still present?
2. When you don't feel God's presence, do you still walk by faith?

WEEK 18
Who Wrestled With Who?

The English might not be grammatically correct, but the meaning is crystal clear

In **Genesis 32:24, 25,** it tells us that Jacob remained alone: and behold a man wrestled with him till morning. When the man saw that he could not win against Jacob, he touched the socket of Jacob's hip so that it was dislocated as they wrestled.

First thing we need to understand is that, names are very important and a name like Jacob isn't something to be proud of. It means heel-catcher or supplanter. That means one who wrongfully or illegally seizes and holds the place of another. In other words, Jacob was one who schemed, connived, plotted and deceived as he traveled down life's road. He did this in order to try to benefit and better himself. Instead of trusting the Lord for His best, he tried to work things out this way. Like many people, often they want what is good (happiness, security, freedom, a bright future, a good marriage, etc.) but they try to obtain what is good in the wrong way. He was a schemer and a trickster.

This mini sharing is not about Jacob, but what brought him to the place that he would get into a wrestling match and one he couldn't win. His circumstances often times are our circumstances; the only difference is he was really sick and tired of being sick and tired and probably thought, "I have nothing else to lose."

You see, Jacob had two wrestling matches going on at this time in his life. One in his mind which was with him all the time and now one with a man. We know who this man was; it was the Lord Jesus Christ who came to put an end to the internal wrestling match of Jacob.

You know, if Jacob had won he would have really lost, but since he lost, he had really won.

The Word of God says a man wrestled with Jacob. Really! How many times has The Lord wrestled with us and had to bring us to that point where we say, I have nothing else to lose, I am not going to let You go until you change you.

The hard thing about our personal reality is that it's so personal and we can't run away from it.

So here we have it, Jacob knew what his name meant and he knew inside who and what he was. He knew that God wasn't pleased with his life because he wasn't pleased with his own life. All of his life was filled with words like schemed, connived, plotted and deceived. That kind of a life has to take a toll on your spiritual life, especially when you have the kind of relatives that Jacob had.

Jacob was finally left alone. That means by himself, which means you can't fool yourself any more. There's no place to run and no place to hide. Its reality time and you are at the bottom of the barrel and the battle in your mind is out of control.

Here's a look at the inner battle that Jacob had because I've had the same battle in my personal life. Lord, I'm sick and tired of this old nature. It's like a roller coaster ride, sometimes up and many times down. How can you be pleased with me, I'm not pleased with me and I really need your help in making a permanent change. I'm tired of the old me and need a new me. I mean the things that I want to do, I don't do them and the things that I really don't want to do, I find myself doing them, what is wrong with me?

Does this battle sound familiar?

So who shows up but the Lord Himself, and here's the battle. Jacob or us, say I'm a nothing and the Lord says you are something. I'm a no-body, you are a some-body. I can do nothing; you can do all things through me. I'm a loser, you are a winner. In other words, this man is wrestling with us. The Lord is trying to bring us to that point that we begin to see ourselves as God sees us.

But we are so set in our negative thinking that the Lord says I will have to touch his strongest point to break him. What is your strongest point, your education, your finances, your accumulations, your job? Whatever it is, if it's causing you to have a wrong perspective of who you are, God will have to touch it and break you. Remember, if you win, you lose because it means you will not change, but if you lose, you really win because God now has a hold of you and you will become what He wants you to be.

This is why Jacob said, I have nothing else to lose and I'm not about to let you go, Lord, because I came this far and I need you to change me, bless me Lord with a changed life. At that point, we go from heel-catcher to prince because God gives us a new name. What is your new name?

Prayer: Father, help me to realize that by losing many of my spiritual battles, I fight in my own strength, I actually win, and by winning many of the battles, I fight in my own strength, I lose.

1. Are your thoughts about yourself ever contradictory to what God says about you knowing that God sees you as a winner?
2. Have you ever won an argument when the one you are fighting with is God?

WEEK 19
Why Turn Your Back On Me Now?

Welcome back to the Tea Table my friends. As always, it's great to have you back again. Today's mini-sharing is really something we need to take a close look at and individually try to answer the question that God is presenting to us.

Jeremiah 2:5; "This is what the Lord says: "What fault could your ancestors have found in me? They paid allegiance to worthless idols, and so became worthless to me".

I really like the Amplified version that puts it this way:

Thus says the Lord: "What unrighteousness did your fathers find in Me, that they went far from Me and habitually went after emptiness, falseness, and futility and themselves became fruitless and worthless?"

Clarke's Commentary on the Bible puts the question this way: What iniquity have your fathers found in me - Have they ever discovered anything cruel, unjust, and oppressive in my laws? Anything unkind or tyrannical in my government? Why then have they become idolaters?

There are a few similar questions that scripture confronts us with, such as:

You know in **John 6:67,** there's a similar question that has to do with turning your back on the Lord and leaving. "Then Jesus turned to the Twelve and asked, "Are you also going to leave?"

I've noticed that people don't usually turn their backs on the Lord all at once; they walk away from Him in small tiny steps until they are comfortable in their fallen state.

Romans 1:21; "for although they knew God, they neither glorified him as God nor gave thanks to him, but their thinking became futile and their foolish hearts were darkened."

2 Kings 17:15, "they rejected his decrees and the covenant he had made with their fathers and the warnings he had given them. They followed worthless idols and themselves became worthless. They imitated the nations around them although the LORD had ordered them. 'Do not do as they do,' and they did the things the LORD had forbidden them to do.'"

You know if you take a close look at these verses, it really presents a scary question and one that needs to be answered and shows us the uselessness of following after those things that profit nothing in God's economy.

I mean God is asking a question not only to the audience of a few thousand years ago, but He's directing the same question to us today.

He's asking what unrighteousness or fault or unjust issues your fathers have with Him? In other words, what sinful or wicked or evil issues did they find in Him that would cause them to turn their backs on Him and follow after useless, worthless things.

Not only did they accuse God of unrighteousness or being unjust and having sinful and evil characteristics, but they turned their back on Him and followed after unrighteous and sinful acts themselves. God turns around and says they have become what they practice, already a habit, which means continuing in a particular practice as a result of an ingrained tendency, and therefore went after emptiness, falseness, and futility and themselves, became fruitless and worthless.

I believe they were so much in love with their fruitless, worthless life style and chose not to change that the only thing they could have done to justify their life style was to accuse God of being just like them. In other words they created God in their own image and turned around to say "see, we are not that bad because God is just like us" or even worse, "we are just like God." This is why in **Joshua 24:15,** it tells us: But if you don't want to serve the LORD, then choose today whom you will serve. Even if you choose the gods, your ancestors served on the other side of the Euphrates or the gods of the Amorites in whose land you live, my family and I will still serve the LORD."

You see, following after emptiness, falseness, and futility or calling it for what it is, turning your back on God and all that He represents is a choice. The truth is no one falls away from God all of a sudden, it is process, and if continued becomes easier and easier.

In **1 Kings 18:21** "Elijah went before the people and said, "How long will you waver between two opinions? If the LORD is God, follow him; but if Baal is God, follow him." But the people said nothing."

Supporting this idea of a process can be found in **Micah 4:5.** "All the nations may walk in the name of their gods;

we will walk in the name of the LORD our God for ever and ever."

Each individual is responsible for making their own decision. Example, in **Daniel 3:18,** speaking in response to serve king Nebuchadnezzar and his gods, the young Hebrew boys tell the king: "But even if he does not, we want you to know, O king, that we will not serve your gods or worship the image of gold you have set up."

In other words, what they said was; 'we have decided to follow after those things that are true, those that are honorable, those that are righteous, those things that are pure, those things that are precious, those things that are praiseworthy, deeds of glory and of praise, we will follow after and meditate on these things.' Knowing that these things are not really things, but a person, and that person has a name, and that name is the King of Kings and the Lord of Lords. By the way, I don't know how they did it, but they quoted **Philippians 4:8**.

You see, my friend, following after things that are empty, false, and futile which means barren and ineffectual and worthless will only cause you to become fruitless, ineffectual and worthless, whereas, following after things that are full, complete, true and useful can only cause you to become full, complete, truthful and useful.

What you follow after is what you become intimate with and what you become intimate with defines who you are.

Listen to what **Job** says in chapter **29 verse 4**, Oh, for the days when I was in my prime, when God's intimate friendship blessed my house.

You see my friends, intimacy with God has a great return on your spiritual investment, not like **Job 19:14,** which tells us: My relatives have failed, and my intimate friends have forgotten me.

God will never and has never forgotten you. And He alone is that anchor that holds when your winds and waves become too much for you to handle.

So when the prophet said make your choice this day, he actually gave you a choice to live a life filled with blessings or with curses. Choosing God is choosing blessings, while abandoning or turning your back on God brings curses.

And by the way, God doesn't curse us, the curse is waiting outside of God's umbrella of protection and when you come out from under that protection, guess what's waiting for you? You bet the curses.

The choice is yours, I strongly recommend choosing God, stay under His umbrella of protection and blessings because it's a life filled with adventure, divine presence, mercy, liberty and excitement.

Prayer: Father, help me to understand that when I give you all the choices in life, you will always make the best decision for my life because you have the very best for me.

1. Have you ever come out of God's umbrella of protection by choice and was really sorry you made that decision?
2. Do you really believe that God has the best choices for your life and wants you close to him? If so, what would make you want to leave his side?

Week 20
What Time is it?

I was sitting here at my desk, and for some reason, my mind flashed back to the 1960 movie, 'The Time Machine.' There was one particular scene that stood out more than others, where the time traveler and his machine vanished in to the past. When his two friends walked in to the empty room, the conversation went something like this:

Mrs. Watchett (the housekeeper): Mister Filby, do you think he'll ever return?
Filby (the time traveler's closest and best friend): One cannot choose but wonder. You see, he has all the time in the world.

As I was mediating on Filby's response, I suddenly realized how pre-occupied and caught up this world is with time. As a matter of fact, the number of watches sold worldwide in 2014 was 1,200,000,000 (One billion two hundred million). That's a lot of watches, and if that isn't amazing in of itself, we have time pieces in our iPads, computers, phones, our cars, in every work place, on most walls in most buildings. We are inundated with time and with all types of time movements such as: mechanical, pendulum, quartz, battery, electronic, electric and animated.

A big question becomes what exactly is time? Nearly two and a half thousand years ago, Aristotle contended that, "time is the most unknown of all unknown things," and arguably not much has changed since then. In the simplest of terms, it seems obvious, what time is: it's the ticking of the clock, the turning of the pages of a calendar. But we know these are just the physical manifestations of the underlying concept.

Time my friends is not easy to describe. Different people have different definitions, for example:

Albert Einstein said time is what clocks measure. Physicist John Wheeler said time is what prevents everything from happening at once. Philosopher, Adolf Grünbaum said time is a linear continuum or range of instants. A Medical Dictionary tells us it's a certain period during which something is done and the Encyclopedia Britannica says it's a scale that lacks spatial dimensions

As you see not only does time have many aspects, but it also has different contexts, such as: "Time stood still", "Excuse me, do you have the time" or "It took a very long time" ,"Adolescence is a difficult time" "This is not the first time this has happened", how about "It's time for dinner" or what we hear often when we need a helping hand, "I don't have time right now" or "Clap in time to the music" and the list goes on and on.

The best and most comprehensive overall definition is that offered by Wikipedia: time is a dimension in which events can be ordered from the past through the present into the future, and also the measure of durations of events and the intervals between them.

Clearly, time is not an object or substance we can touch or see. But neither is it merely a dimension, quantity or a concept.

So how do we deal with specific names of time such as past, present and future?

The past may be well-defined as those events which occurred before a given point in time, occasions which are usually considered to be fixed and undisputable or what we call history. The present may be defined as the time connected with the events assumed directly and for the first time, what we call the now. The future is the unknown time period after the present moment

I'm sure some out there are saying to themselves, is there a message somewhere in this or is this a science paper, so bear with me my friends. The truth is, we live in a society bombarded with the concern or interest or even an obsession with time. And it will never, ever be said about us what Mr. Filby said about the time traveler from the Time Machine, and I quote: you see, he has all the time in the world.

My friends, we do not have all the time in the world, and whatever time we have left is limited and running out. And don't be fooled, every second wasted will not and cannot be done over. This is why they say, time waits for no man. One thing I do know is that time is accountable to God. We pass through what we call time, but time has to give an answer to God.

As a matter-of fact, in the book of **Joshua and 2 Kings**, God made time stop and go backwards until God's plan was accomplished.

Don, how can you say that? Because scripture which cannot lie tells us: "For a thousand years in your sight are but as yesterday when it is past, or as a watch in the night." We are also told "…with the Lord one day is as a thousand years, and a thousand years as one day." Isaiah says that God "inhabits eternity that means God populates or lives in eternity or better yet, eternity dwells within God.

When we say things like "God is timeless" or "God has no beginning or end," we are trying to explain God in terms of a dimension by which He is not constrained. God created time so time is accountable to God just as everything in the known and unknown universe is accountable to God or as I like to say, everything in the known and unknown universe is answerable and responsible to God.

The first most important question ever asked was when God walked in the cool of the garden and asked the question: Adam, where are you? Or as the true meaning emerges, Adam, where's your head at, don't you see the immediate and long term consequences of your actions?

So with your hustle, bustle life filled with programs, schedules, going here, going there, doing this, doing that, another very important question to you my friends is: What Time Is It? Because you never know how soon it will become too late.

Prayer: Father, I know a day is like a thousand years and a thousand years is like a day, so when you tell me to wait a second, I know I should sit down because it will take a while. Help me to be patient when waiting on you and to understand that you are working out the details in my life.

1. Do you have a hard time waiting on the Lord or do you want everything done yesterday? Why is that?
2. When the Lord tells you to hurry up and wait, do you try to help him in the decision process? If yes, did everything work out exactly the way you wanted it to work out?
3. Does the expression, I don't have time to do it right the first time, but end up having time to do it right the second time mean anything to you? Why?

Week 21
Reflections

Most teachings are great, but I personally find the best teachings as the ones that cause you to take a look at your life and make the necessary changes that need to be made. I guess you would call that one of life's self-exams.

Today's teaching is such a lesson and I pray it helps you as it's helping me. Did you notice I said helping and not helped? That means some lessons in life take a long time, just like working out our sanctification takes a long time, an entire lifetime to be exact.

You know, when a non-smoker comes in contact with a heavy smoker, they know it almost immediately. And don't get me wrong, I have nothing against smokers. I always say a smoker can smoke and still go to heaven; the only difference is they will probably get there faster.
So how does a non-smoker know if the other person is a smoker? Because of the smell. It's on their clothes, their skin, their breath, in their hair. As a matter-of-fact, you probably don't even have to see the person because the smell greets you before the actual contact.

Heavy drinkers have the same affect. You can smell the alcohol on their breath not to mention their behavior when under the influence. Staggering, in some cases, falling down and in many cases, abnormal behavior of becoming verbally or even physically abusive to their mates or others they come in contact with.

Smokers and alcoholics don't have a monopoly on strange and erratic behavior. Drug users or individuals that abuse medications also do strange things.

Obviously, this isn't a teaching on the vices we find in public, but a teaching on behavior when something has been poured out into our lives. In other words, when we have been exposed to a large dose of anything in life, our life will reflect what it is we have been exposed to. It can be anything from tobacco, alcohol, drugs, money, and excessive work to even things that are meant to help us, like chemo-therapy. There is always a reflection in our lives of some things that have been poured out into our lives, which brings me to the heart of the message.

We are told in **Romans 5:5;** and hope does not put us to shame, because God's love has been poured into our hearts through the Holy Spirit who has been given to us.

Did you hear that? It didn't just say love, but God's love and that it has been poured into our hearts through the Holy Spirit. Not only that, but we also have come to know and to believe the love that God has for us. God is love, and whoever abides in love abides in God, and God abides in him according to **1 John 4:16**.

A great self-examination question to ask ourselves is: if a smoker or alcoholic or drug user or anything which has become evident in our lives, because of exposure can be manifested in our everyday activities, what about the love of God. If the love of God has been poured into our hearts the question that has to arise is, does my life reflect the love of God?

Is my attitude, speech, behavior and conduct evidence that God's love has found a dwelling place in my heart? We are told in **1 Corinthians 13:4-8,** "Love is patient and kind; love does not envy or boast; it is not arrogant or rude. It does not insist on its own way; it is not irritable or resentful; it does not rejoice at wrongdoing, but rejoices with the truth. Love bears all things, believes all things, hopes all things, and endures all things. Love never ends." As a matter-of-fact, according to the Word of God, let all that you do be done in love, **1 Corinthians 16:14**. Not just some of the things we do, but all that we do and everything we do should reflect the love of God that has already been poured out into our hearts.

Jesus was once asked a question, "Teacher, which is the great commandment in the Law?" And he said to him, "You shall love the Lord your God with all your heart and with all your soul and with all your mind. This is the first and greatest commandment. And the second is like it: You shall love your neighbor as yourself. All the Law and Prophets depend on these two commandments. **Matthew 22:36-40**.

You see, my friend, the first and second most important questions have to do with love. Why? Why is love that important? The answer is because anyone who does not love does not know God, because God is love **1 John 4:8** and if love has been poured into our hearts, it's the same as God has been poured into our hearts, and with that much presence of God in our hearts, there has to be a manifested evidence that we are vessels of God's presence. Truth be told, if you want to live in joy or peace or harmony, it can only be done through the love of God and not your own efforts or works.

Are you sure about that, Don? Well, **Colossians 3:14,** tells me, and above all these put on love, which binds everything together in perfect harmony. Did you hear that, love binds everything together in perfect harmony?

Let me just say one more thing. Walking in the love of God doesn't mean you have to be a battering ram or throw rug for every situation that comes your way. It doesn't mean that you have to give in to every situation that you are confronted with nor does it mean that you always have to give up on your dreams so others can get their way. It means in all situations, you are to be the reflection of the invisible Jesus, just as Jesus was the reflection of the invisible Father. Granted, situations will arise in your life that are not your first choice and you may want to re-act to the wrongs that happen, but remember **Romans 12:19,** beloved, never avenge yourselves, but leave it to the wrath of God, for it is written, "Vengeance is mine, I will repay, says the Lord."

Prayer: Father, help me to be the reflection of the invisible Jesus, even as Jesus was the reflection of the invisible Father, and to bloom where I'm planted.

1. When you first get up in the morning and you look in the mirror, do you like the image that is looking

back at you, knowing the type of person God has
called you to be?

2. Do you believe the trials and tribulations of life can
    distort the image you see in the mirror? How do
    you clean a dirty mirror?

Week 22
Oh Lord, So Much to Do, so Little Time

I remember when I was a youngster living in Florida, and more than once while out walking in the fields by our house I would stumble across a fire ants nest mound. Everyone in South Florida and probably all of Florida knew immediately what a fire ant's nest looked like, a mound about 10 inches high and maybe a foot in diameter and made up of what looked like granular powder.

The intelligent people and victims of a fire ant sting would immediately make an about-face and walk away because they knew the sting of a fire ant was excruciating, which means agonizing and extremely painful, not to mention the sting would leave welts that itched and lasted for many, many days.

Anyway, not always, but every once in a while when I came across one of these mounds, it was as if I couldn't control my urge and I would quickly, very quickly, kick the mound with my foot and scatter the mound. Almost immediately, hundreds and hundreds of fire ants would come streaming out of the hole in the ground ready for battle. Of course, I immediately stepped back to a safe distance and watched what seemed like total and complete chaos.

If you watched closely and knew what you were looking for, you would notice some ants immediately went to protect the eggs, other ants would immediately start to rebuild the mound, others would try to save the food that was gathered up and others were looking for who or whatever disturbed their mound with the intent of leaving serious welts as a reminder never to do that again.

Interestingly, I've seen that ant's nest activity in some of the homes of believers. Trying to juggle life in the home, the family, the job, personal life, church activities, school and so many other issues that the cry of their heart becomes; Oh Lord, so much to do and so little time.

It reminded me of a story I once heard about a woman who spent 8 hours a day cleaning the house, but nothing seemed to get done. When questioned, she said; I don't understand it, I clean the house from the time my husband goes to work in the morning until he returns in the evening and nothing ever looks done or neat. What does your day look like, asked her friend? Well, as soon as Bob leaves for work, I start to clean the breakfast dishes, but I notice there's a broom next to the washer which reminds me to sweep the floor, so I leave the dishes and start sweeping the floor until I notice a shirt hanging on a chair which reminds me to do the laundry, so I leave the sweeping to start the laundry, only to notice some cookies on a plate from last night's guests, which reminds me I have to make a food list for shopping, so I put the laundry on hold to do the food shopping, but on the way to the supermarket, I remembered to drop off a book at the library and on and on and on until at the end of the day, I'm exhausted and nothing is done. So much to do and so little time.

There was a woman once that we all know of and can relate to, some better than others I'm sure, and I speculate that Martha was busy cooking and setting the dishes and watching the oven so the food wouldn't get burned and wanting to please her very special guest, the one they call Jesus, this amazing person that could perform miracles and that crowds of people would follow just to hear His words. I'm sure she must have thought to herself, I want to hear what He's saying, but my lazy sister, Mary, isn't doing a thing to help me; she just sits at His feet and listens to what He's saying. Who's supposed to take care of all these chores? I'm not going to do it alone, that's for sure, not with so much to do and so little time.

Out of complete frustration mixed with probably anger for her lazy sister, Mary, she breaks on the scene and says in **Luke 10:40,** But Martha was distracted with much serving, and she approached Him and said, Lord, do You not care that my sister has left me to serve alone? Therefore, tell her to help me.

Sometimes, life can really be a drain on our physical wellbeing and certainly, our spiritual life. Many of you Mom's, know what it's like to be distracted with serving, planning, working, studying and raising children, as well as being the help mate to your spouse, and it's even worse if you have teenagers that have no idea what it's like to chip in and help out at the house.

And you husbands, many of you know what it's like to be a workaholic, leave the house early in the morning for the office, work all day just to come home later than usual because a task needs to be completed on time. You also try to juggle life as we know it, to be the best Dad you can be and the perfect husband you can be and the spiritual head of the family, and also try to be the bread winner so you can support the family in all their areas of need.

It reminds me of a graduate school paper I once wrote entitled; The Ladder of Success. Rather than go in to all the detail of the term paper, it boiled down to this: what happens when you reach the top of the ladder of success only to find the ladder was leaning on the wrong wall?

You know the picture, the Dad having worked 12 hours a day, six days a week for most of his life, now the CEO of the company, seven digit income, 6 bedroom house with swimming pool and tennis court next to the four car garage that houses the BMW's, Mercedes and Corvette. At the very top of the ladder of success, but looking back at what expenses? The kids are into drugs, having been kicked out of college. Your only friends are the ones who remain friends as long as you continue to help them in every way. You sit at one end of the 48 place dinner table and your wife sits at the other end so very far away. But you made it, you are at the top of the ladder of success, and yet you are not at peace but pieces. There is something very wrong with this picture.

Just to be clear, can a person be at the top of the ladder of success and still have an intimate relationship with the family and with God? Of course, **Deuteronomy 8:18** says, "And you shall remember the Lord your God, for it is He who gives you power to get wealth." **Psalm 5:12** "For You, O Lord, will bless the righteous; with favor You will surround him as with a shield." **Proverbs 3:5 & 6** tells us, "Trust in the Lord with all your heart, and lean not on your own understanding; in all your ways acknowledge Him, and He shall direct your paths." Notice it says paths, not path. One is singular and the other is plural or many paths.

My friends, the blessings of the kingdom can only come about through obedience to the King of the kingdom.

God always blesses obedience. Not only are you blessed but the blessings of God will come upon you and overtake you. In **Deuteronomy 28**, we are told when you are obedient to the voice of your God, you will be blessed in the city (your home), in the country (your nation) , blessed in the fruit of your body (health), the produce of your ground (what you put your hand to, including your job) with increase of your herds (belongings), the offspring of your flocks (what continues after you), your basket (what you already have), your kneading bowl (what you will have) and the blessing; just go on and on and on. Why? Because you dare to be obedient to what God is telling you.

Besides, it's hard to sit at the feet of Jesus when you are at the top of a ladder. Not only is the distance from the top of the ladder to the feet of Jesus a long way off, but it's also very hard to hear what Jesus is saying when you are far away.

I once heard; if you feel far from God, it's because someone moved. Let me repeat that, if you feel far from God, it's because someone moved.

So what is the answer to the cry of; so much to do and so little time to do it or what do I do with all the distraction of life?

The answer can be found in the paraphrased **Luke 10:39,** And Martha had a sister called Mary who sat at the feet of Jesus, which was the one and good thing to do, so she could hear what Jesus had to say.

And that my friends is the key to life, sit at the feet of Jesus and hear what He has to say.

Prayer: Lord, help me to be better at my time management and to put you first and not last because I never know how soon it will be too late.

1. Do you sometimes put Jesus on the back burner or on the shelf because you have so many things that are so much more important?
2. The things that you consider to be so much more important, are they really that important and take priority over spending time with the Lord?

Week 23
Who or What's in Control?

Have you ever noticed that every once in a while, we are confronted with a situation that is so obvious that we are almost forced to express our personal opinion on the issue staring us right in the eyes?

I've spoken with a number of people, Christian and non-Christian and it seems that everyone has an opinion concerning the Presidential race between the Republican and Democratic nominees for the next President of the United States.

Trust me, I've heard it all and I'm sure you have too and probably have expressed many of the same sentiments yourself as I must confess, so have I.

How many have heard or thought to yourself, I would never vote for a person who's a liar, deceitful and acts as if he or she is above the law. I would hate to have that person as a president, so arrogant, filled with self-pride and has no control over his or her mouth and says just about anything that comes to mind.

I've heard a number of people say, if that person becomes president, our country and government will go right down the tubes and our great country will lose all credibility to the rest of the world. I've even heard some say, what's the difference, most of the presidents were corrupt, dishonest and concerned with fame, fortune and lime-light and not the American people, the only difference was some got caught and others did not.

Granted, much of what's being expressed or spoken out loud or even thought about is probably true and will probably continue way past our lifetime and for all practical purposes, will most likely get even worse.

How can this be allowed to continue, you might be thinking?

Ask yourself the question, what is a president or a government official or any person that walks the face of the earth, but a human being. The truth is, if you're putting your eyes on the government to help bail you out of a situation or help take care of your needs, then, my friends, you've got your eyes on the wrong government. In the same way, if you've got your eyes on a person to deliver you from a situation or to make your life or the life of your family better, then you have your eyes on the wrong deliverer.

We are told in **Isaiah 51:12** "I, yes I, am the one who comforts you. So why are you afraid of mere humans, who wither like the grass and disappear? The reality is that presidents don't become presidents on their own accord, meaning whoever becomes the next president of the United States didn't get that position by mistake or luck or even in their own strength. Thank God for **Daniel 2:21**, He (meaning God) controls the course of world events; he removes kings and sets up other kings. He gives wisdom to the wise and knowledge to the scholars. You see, God raises up kings or presidents and removes kings or presidents and there in no one that can stop Him, no person

101

or group or government. We are told in **Psalms 115:3,**
"Our God is in heaven. He does whatever he wants."

You see, my friend, you might not like the candidate that's
running for president for whatever reason, and you might
be correct for those reasons, but all your complaints is not
going to change the outcome because God is in control of
the elections and He will put whichever person He wants
into the Oval Office. If you don't believe me, just take a
look at the Old Covenant and see which kings ruled over
Israel. Most of them were really evil, but God raised them
up for a purpose and for a season. In **Ecclesiastes 3:1,** we
are comforted with "There is an appointed time for
everything. And there is a time for every event under
heaven." That appointed time and event is set by the King
of Glory who knows the ending from the beginning and not
us or our election system or government officials.
Remember, God does whatever He pleases with whoever
He chooses for whatever time He decides. If that were not
true, why would we be told in **Romans 13:1** that, every
person must be subject to the governing authorities, for no
authority exists except by God's permission? The existing
authorities have been established by God,

So a good question to keep in our mind while all this
foolishness is going on during the elections would be: Who
or what's in Control?

Another good question would be, so what's my
responsibility in the midst of all this? First of all, your
responsibility is not to drop out, but to step up to the
challenge and pray for wisdom.

You see, I believe most Christians in America seem to think that God has given general principles of right and wrong in the Bible and that He expects us to rely primarily on our own wisdom and reason when choosing a president, and nothing is further from the truth. The Bible provides very clear instructions that should guide us in voting for a president, and we are responsible to God for our decision to accept or reject those instructions.

Proverbs 16:2 tells us "All a person's ways seem right in his own opinion, but the LORD evaluates the motives." Meaning everyone has an opinion on how to vote in this election and they will think that their opinion is right, but ultimately, it is God and not man who will decide which vote is the right vote to cast. In other words, we cannot trust our own reason and thoughts because our hearts are deceitful and desperately wicked according to **Jeremiah 17:9**. If that's true, how should we determine who to vote for if we cannot trust our own reason and thoughts?

The answer can be found in **Proverbs 3:5, 6,** which says, "Trust in the LORD with all your heart and do not lean on your own understanding. In all your ways, acknowledge Him, and He will make your paths straight."

So as a Christian, our responsibility is to seek the Lord, get all the information you can about each candidate, seek the Lord again and ask for His guidance in voting and vote. Realizing that you are doing what God asks of you and He will have the final say about who becomes the next leader of this great country, and He, and only He will bring about His plans.

Finally and according to Robert Driskell, Christians should not have a rebellious, antagonistic attitude toward our leaders. Nothing happens that God does not authorize. Therefore, those politicians who are in power are there because God has allowed it. History has shown us that, generally, a people who are following God will have good leaders, whereas a people who reject God will have ungodly leaders. Oftentimes, it is through these ungodly leaders that God's judgment is felt on those who have rejected Him.

What do we do with our government, regardless of which party is elected? The answer can be found in **1 Timothy 2:1, 2**. I urge you, first of all, to pray for all people. Ask God to help them; intercede on their behalf, and give thanks for them. Pray this way for kings (and I might add for presidents and all government officials) and all who are in authority so that we can live peaceful and quiet lives marked by godliness and dignity, and this, my friend, is good and pleasing in the sight of God our Savior.

Prayer: Father, help me to realize that the earth and everything in it and on it belongs to you and that I keep my eyes on you, regardless of how things seem to be or where they are going, and that you are high and lifted up seated on the throne of heaven and are not running for re-election.

1. Do you ever think to yourself, if I were God I wouldn't do things that way, I would do it this way? Does your way always turn out to be the right way?

2. When scripture tells us that Jesus is the King of Kings and Lord of Lords, can you honestly say that He is absolutely your King and Lord over everything you do?

Week 24
This Very Day

The other day, I was reading in the book of **Ezekiel 24:2** and verse 2 just jumped off the page and really got my attention. When I say that it got my attention, I mean it was as if a mighty breath of wind slammed in to my understanding.

Here we have God speaking to the son of man and just in case you forgot, we who are believers in Christ fall into the same classification as son of man. And God tells Ezekiel; write down the name of this day, this very day. Be sure my friends, God was not saying jot down if it's Thursday or Tuesday or even a Sunday. For some, we can proudly proclaim and say this is the day the LORD has made. We will rejoice and be glad in it. Another way of stating that is: the LORD has done it this very day; let us rejoice today and be glad.

As a side note, I'm sure some are thinking what about women? The Hebrew expression "son of man" (אדם־בן, ben-'adam) is used primarily as a form of address as in the Book of Ezekiel or to contrast the lowly status of humanity against the permanence and gloried dignity of God, so son of man carries the same weight as daughter of man since we are all creations of God, but children of men.

You know, the weight that the expression this very day carries is a heavy weight and carries with it the accumulation of many years and decisions.

I was reading about the ISIS attack in Paris France and for 127 plus lives, this very day was the day that they lost their lives to terrorism. When those 127 people stand before the Mercy Seat of God and He says what did you write down for the name of this day, this very day. What a scary thought! For all them, they will have to say this was the day we lost our lives, left our loved ones, husbands, wives and children, never to return to them in this life. For some, they might say this is the day I met my Lord face to face, this very day.

You know, we all have one thing in common, saved and unsaved, and that is, we are all one breath away from eternity. While we are still alive and able to enjoy the smell of fresh air, feel the sun shining on our faces, enjoy our friends and the days, as they tick off to that day, that very day when we are taken home. For the saved, a day of graduation and celebration, for the unsaved, a day of weeping and gnashing of teeth, and thank God that I don't know what that day, that very day is, but there is a day that has my name on it and a day that has your name on it. For some, it may be closer than they think and for others, it may be a long way off.

Thanks be to a gracious, compassionate, merciful, loving heavenly Father who doesn't want us pre-occupied and focusing on when that day comes, but wants us to realize that the days He has given us are not to be wasted on meaningless living but on bringing Him glory.

Each one of us can answer our own question that asks: on this day, this very day did I bring glory to God? Did I do what was right in His eyes or did I do what was right in my own eyes? On this day, this very day was I more concerned about pleasing God or pleasing myself?

The Apostle Paul once made a statement that I'm sure I have said on many occasions; on this day, this very day the things I want to do I don't do and yet the very things I don't want to do, those are the things that I do. But I can also say that this day, this very day, I am closer to my Lord than I was yesterday, but not as close as I will be tomorrow. Why can I say that? Because I don't have to be a genius to realize that walking and staying close to my Lord is the most important thing that I can do in life.

As my vertical relationship with God increases, my horizontal relationship with people increases. In other words, the more time I spend with my heavenly Father, hear His voice and seek His face and not His hand, the deeper the level of my intimacy with Him grows, and as that happens, I am filled with His presence, and therefore, this day, this very day I can be poured out to a needy world and make a difference to at least one person that needs to hear a word of encouragement or hope or edification or that God is real and there is a wonderful life filled with the presence of God and that all the pain and suffering going on in the world, although real, doesn't have to be experienced alone.

So my question to you is: this day, this very day, what is the testimony that this day will say about you? Was this a day where you walked closer to God than you did yesterday? Was this a day where you showed the love of

God to your family your children your spouse? Was this a day that put a smile on the face of God as He walked with you in places that He was manifested through you that brought glory to God and hope to some of His creation?

The next question for you becomes: when you hear Son of man, write down the name of this day, this very day, what will your response be?

Prayer: Oh God, I know my days on this earth are all numbered in your book, but help me to live each day to the fullest and to enjoy your presence regardless of what's going on around me.

1. Are you glad that God hasn't told you the very day that he would take you home to be with him? Why?
2. Do you ever think about the time that you have wasted on things that profit you nothing and you have nothing to show for it? How can you start to make your time Godly?

Week 25
My Way, Your Way

More than once when I have been going down a rocky
road, and no, I don't mean the ice cream, I usually end up
stopping and try to gather my senses as to where I'm at and
why are things going the way they are going for me.

This is usually a great opportunity for me to be honest with
myself and to take a self-exam as to the methods that got
me to where I'm at. Let's face it; we all are responsible for
our actions and the consequences that follow our actions.

I remember in college my physics professor telling me I
can either do the detailed experiments my way or I can do it
the right way. That's when I learned the expression that I
don't have time to do it right the first time, but always have
time to do it right the second time.

It kind of reminds me of the song made famous by Frank
Sinatra called; My Way

And now, the end is near; and so I face the final curtain.
My friend, I'll say it clear, I'll state my case, of which I'm
certain.
I've lived a life that's full. I've traveled each and every
highway;
And more, much more than this, I did it my way.

A few things in the song are very true, we will all face the
final curtain one day and we have no idea how near the end
is or how soon it will be too late. And granted, some may

110

have lived a fuller life than others and some may have travelled more highways than others, but the part of the song that usually gets us in trouble is, we did it our way.

It is hard to follow someone if you are going your own way. I remember this one day at the Space Center in Florida when it was pouring rain. I mean the heavens opened up and it was a torrential flood coming down, but I didn't have an umbrella. A fellow engineer said I could walk under his large beach umbrella, and so, we both started off. At a close distance to the car, I turned right and my friend went straight and I got soaking wet. I complained, what are you doing? My car is over there. He said you were going your way, but I was going my way. In other words, I came out from under the protection of his umbrella because we were both going in different ways. He went his way and I went my way, and in order for me to stay dry, his way had to be my way.

How many times has the Lord told us to follow Him and we do for a distance until we get close to what we think is our goal and then we go our way and do it our way only to find it was the wrong way? We read in scripture; and he said to them, "Follow me, and I will make you fishers of men." **Matthew 4:19**. They were already fishermen doing it their way, but the Lord says now I want you to do it My way.

I really love the story in **Luke 5**. He saw at the water's edge two boats, left there by the fishermen, who were washing their nets. He got into one of the boats, the one belonging to Simon, and asked him to put out a little from

111

shore. Then he sat down and taught the people from the boat. When he had finished speaking, he said to Simon, "Put out into deep water, and let down the nets for a catch." Simon answered, "Master, we've worked hard all night and haven't caught anything. But because you say so, I will let down the nets." When they had done so, they caught such a large number of fish that their nets began to break. So they signaled their partners in the other boat to come and help them, and they came and filled both boats so full that they began to sink, **Luke 5: 2-7**. I can just imagine Jesus telling Peter to let down the nets and Peter could have said, Lord, you just don't understand, I'm a professional fishermen and been doing it my way for years. You see, there's your way of doing things and the right way, which is the Lord's way.

Just because you have diplomas and degrees hanging on the wall or just because you have success in the bank doesn't mean your way is the only way. Peter was an experienced fisherman, but he was teachable and because he was open to change, he did it Jesus's way, which turned out to be the successful way.

Doing it your own way almost always seems to come about when a decision has to be made. You know what I mean; a car has to be purchased or a new home or which school to put the children in or what are you going to pick up at the department store, and I'm sure the list goes on and on. It's a decision that has to be made. There's nothing wrong in making decisions, the problem is what steps you used to come to the final decision. I mean, did you do what you did based on a gut feeling or it just seemed right or you had a warm fuzzy that it was the right thing to do?

We are told; trust in the Lord with all your heart, and do not lean on your own understanding. In all your ways acknowledge him, and he will make straight your paths **Proverbs 3:5-6**. Not to acknowledge Him in all your ways is the same as doing it your own way.

I've come to the place in my understanding where I realize that I have absolutely no idea what tomorrow is going to bring in my life. I can assume what may happen tomorrow based on some decisions that I've made today, but the reality is I have absolutely no idea. Based on that statement why would I want to lean on my own understanding for doing things my own way when I'm told the heart of man plans his way, but the Lord establishes his steps. **Proverbs 16:9.** If the Lord says He is going to plan my steps I'm pretty sure He doesn't need my help, but my obedience, and when I give all the choices to God for my future, I'm sure He will make the very best decisions for my life.

There's a verse that is so very true, although every verse in the bible is true, but this one really drives home a point that doing it your own way is not necessarily the right way and it tells us: come now, you who say, "Today or tomorrow, we will go to a particular town, spend a year there, while trading and making profit"— yet, you do not know what tomorrow will bring. What is your life? For you are a mist that appears for a little time and then vanishes. Instead, you ought to say, "If the Lord wills, we will live and do this or that." **James 4:13-15**.

My friend, how many times have you done it your own way only to find it was the wrong way and you had to go back and do whatever it was all over again? And who knows how much time and effort and expense was involved in having to do it your way when the Lord could have showed you the correct way and saved you all that time, effort and expense.

In closing, God tells us for I know the plans I have for you," declares the LORD, "plans to prosper you and not to harm you, plans to give you hope and a future. **Jeremiah 29:11**.

That word, know, means God is already acquainted with what He has in store for your entire life. The word plans means He has in place the devices and purposes that He will use to bring about your success. That word, prosper means completeness in safety, health, prosperity, peace, friendship, tranquility, contentment and welfare. That phrase not to harm you means God doesn't want any disagreeable, malignant, unpleasant, evil, bad, unkind, unhappy, vicious, sad thing to be part of your life. One more thing, God doesn't want to give you hope in the future, but hope and a future.

What is the future? My friend, for each of us, the future is what's beyond us right now. God wants to give us an expectation of what's coming next in to our lives and that it be filled with all the good things that God has in store for us, and all He wants is for us to rely and trust in His decisions for our life and not try to get through life by doing it our own way. God truly wants our latter days, which means our final days to be greater than our former days, and that word, greater, in Hebrew is "Gadol" which means: superior, magnificent, awe-inspiring, and filled with greatness and might. And that, my friend, is what God wants for you and for me today and forever

Prayer: Lord, help me to make Godly choices in life, knowing there is my way and your way, and your ways have never failed me yet.

1. In making decisions in life, have you ever found your way to be better than the Lord's way? Why do you think doing it your way might be the right way?

Week 26
As the Occasion Demands

I remember when I was just a kid living in New York City, my older brother and I had the opportunity to go to camp at a place called Bear Mountain in up-state New York, which was in the middle of the woods. We weren't used to so many trees and the feeling of being alone in nature without the sounds of cars and just plain noise. Amazing, our Mom took us out of the city with the hectic life style of the city, but we couldn't take the city out of ourselves.

Anyway, we had an opportunity for the two of us to go in a canoe in this rather large lake, although the area where we were was completely roped off for our safety. There we were, me in the front with my paddle and my brother in the rear with his paddle. Great combination you might be thinking, wrong. I wanted to go to a small island in the middle of the lake and my brother wanted to go to a clump of trees on the other end of the shore. Thinking back on what this scene must have looked like would have caused anyone to roll over with laughter. There I was in the front rowing as hard as I could, splashing all over the place and there my brother was in the rear of the canoe paddling in the opposite direction, also splashing all over the place. Bottom line, there was a lot of splashing, but not an inch of travel and this went on for almost 15 minutes until it turned into a duel of paddles standing up in the canoe until the canoe flipped over and the adventure was over. Thank God we were both very good swimmers.

This scene brought to mind a verse from **Amos 3:3** which tells us; can two people walk together without agreeing on the direction? Granted, in our case, it would have read; can two brothers row together without agreeing on the direction and the answer would have to be no, absolutely not.

How can two people agree on doing anything unless there's some form of agreement on what you are doing and where you are going? In the Hebrew, when you take a closer look at **Amos 3:3** it means more than just going someplace, the word walk means a manner of life and together means a union or unitedness. The word together means much more than we agree, but is like a union or to betroth. So Amos is really telling us: how can two people reach a destination unless their manner of life is betrothed in a union together to the agreement of the destination.

Why **Amos 3:3**? Because we as believers desire to be used by God in signs and wonders. We sometimes even dream about laying hands on someone and watching as the blind see and the deaf hear or speaking a word and the lame jump up and walk as in the case of **Acts 3:8**; He, the crippled man jumped to his feet and began to walk. Then he went with them into the temple courts, walking and jumping, and praising God, and all because an obedient man of God seized the crippled man by the right hand, raised him up; and immediately, the crippled man's feet and ankles were strengthened.

Most of us would have loved to be used by God for a time such as this. The wonderful thing about that is, God

117

Himself would also love for us to be that person to be used by Him as well, for the very same kind of miracles.

So God is in agreement and we are in agreement that we want to be used for signs and wonders on the earth. We also have a destination, which in this case is the miraculous signs and wonders amongst people for healings, deliverance and setting the captives free. Again, God agrees with us on this destination and we both agree that we would like this to be a manner of life with us. So **Amos 3:3** belongs to us because we meet all the qualifications of walking together, agreeing on the same thing and our destination is one and the same, namely, people.

I said all of that as an introduction to a wonderful verse which is found in **1 Samuel 10:7** and let it be, when these signs come to you, that you do as the occasion demands; for God is with you.

When you get a gut feeling (desire, inclination, leading) to lay hands on a sick person or pray for a needy individual or maybe a name or face pops into your mind seemingly out of no-where and you have a sudden need to lift that person up, what do you think that gut feeling is and where do you think it came from? That my friend, is a sign and that sign came from the Lord.

How many times have you been at a certain place and you see a person in a wheel chair, suddenly, you develop a gut feeling that you would like to see that person be able to get up out of that wheel chair and even more than that, that you would like to be the instrument that God uses to enable that person to get up?

Do we do it? Usually not. Why? Lots of reasons, like fear of failure, too many people around and if it doesn't work, they will all see, giving the individual in the wheel chair hope and then letting him down because he didn't get healed. Maybe you're not sure if you were really hearing from the Lord and it would have been easier if you had a really, really big sign from heaven that you are to go and do it.

Let me put your mind at ease, there are three things I've personally learned and I'm 100% sure it applies to you as well. I can't heal anyone, I can't save anyone and I can do both 1 and 2 through Jesus, and without Jesus, the only thing I can do well is "fail".

You see my friends, having that sign or gut feeling to be used by God to heal or get someone saved isn't something that is born from your inner man, it isn't something that your mind is constantly fixed on day and night while you go through the hectic paces of what we call life. When that desire does come upon you, learn to trust that it is actually a sign from God because God desires to use you as an instrument to bring about signs and wonders right there and then.

When you do come to that place of knowing that it's from God and that only through God can you actually do it and you claim **1 Samuel 10:7** when these signs come to you, that you do as the occasion demands; for God is with you, use the sign as an opportunity to meet the demand of the occasion and fear not because, you can't heal anyone and you can't save anyone, while God can, and God is with you, so you can't fail and allow God to use you as the vessel to gets His work done, knowing that He and only He will get all the glory, the honor and the praise.

Prayer: Lord, help me to be aware of the open doors that you open and to say yes when you present the occasion to be obedient to your voice.

1. Have you ever found yourself going in one direction when the Lord was going in the opposite direction? Why was it so difficult to turn around and follow God?
2. Have there been times when the Lord presented an occasion to be obedient and you said no, I want to do it my way? What happened?

Week 27
A Time Long Ago

The Lord woke me up at 3:00 in the morning with my mind just racing with thoughts and images. There was so much mental activity going on that there was no way I could have gone back to sleep. Not only that, but there was no way I could let all those thoughts and images go unrecorded.

If you are reading this devotional, it can mean only one thing, you my friend, yes you, are still alive and not gone.

As I lay upon my bed early in the morning, lying there in the dark with just the sound of the fan, I found myself remembering events and people from different times in my childhood. A face would pop into my mind, then a name and best of all, a chapter of my life with things we did together as kids.

Interesting enough, my mind couldn't differentiate between when I was eight or nine or when I was a teenager, it would just recall the great, memorable times we had together with different people, best friends of a time long ago. How long ago? A time when you could leave your door unlocked at night and not worry. A time when most televisions were black and white and sat in a wooden cabinet that was enormous. A time when all the music on the radio could be understood and best of all, a time when you could buy milk and bread and still get change back from the dollar you handed the man behind the counter and gay meant you were happy and queer meant you were odd and comedians were funny without using foul language.

One scene not solicited but relived in my mind was at Play land, an amusement park where I would go with my elder brothers and my best friends, and what a great time we had there and what fun just remembering those times. As I lay there in the early morning darkness, I was able to smell the popcorn in the air and the hot dogs, and the sound of the wooden roller coaster in the background, my goodness, smells of my childhood that shook my memory like a tidal wave of joyful thoughts.

Then as quickly as it came, the memory vanished only to be replaced with another amazing and wonderful memory of a different time of so long ago. I remembered as a teenager, me and my best friends all sitting in a convertible driving down main street with the oldest of our little 'rat-pack' driving, the only one that legally could drive and with the car top down. I was being inundated with feelings, sights and sounds, and oh yes, the smells again as I remembered how the air was blowing our hair and the warm feeling of the sun beating down on us, all eight of us in one car, five in the back seat and three in the front seat. Radio blasting out a song from the Platters and all of us singing at the top of our lungs, what a great time it was. Music with words you could understand with a theme that made sense and names like Nat King Cole, Perry Como and oh yes, Frank Sinatra .

As I recalled in my mind all these incredible images with friends and faces from my past and aromas that went with the mental experiences that I was reliving, it began to dawn on me that there was a reason for what I was experiencing and it was a lot more than just having a good feeling, it was more than God being really, really nice to me and letting me have these memories.

I would recall a face and all of a sudden, it dawned on me, that person, that best friend is gone, that face has passed on. Then another face and experience would pop up and again, wait a second, that person has also passed away, as a matter of fact, that family member has also died and is gone.

This is why I opened this teaching with; if you are listening or reading this teaching, it can mean only one thing, you my friend, yes you, are still alive and not gone.

The idea came to me that as long as I have great and fond memories of events and friends of so long ago, that the person is not really gone, but continues to live in my mind. Even with that, I could hear myself asking me the question; what difference does it make? I realize my present is made up of all my past experiences, which includes the faces of friends, living and dead, smells, scenes, actions and places, and well, let's face it, everything that it took to get me to where I am today.

So the question now became; what difference am I making? I certainly can't make a difference to those who have passed on but I can make a difference to the rest of the people that I come in contact with each and every day. So to add to the; what difference am I making I now ask, what kind of a difference and how will I be remembered when I'm gone?

My friends, if all I did was to help you have a great memory, although it may put a smile on your face, in the scope of life, what difference did that really make? Did it help you become spiritually closer to God?

Did it strengthen in your life the need to establish an intimate relationship with Jesus or how to be a better Mother or Father or how to take God more seriously or how to be all you can be as a child of the Living God?

Listen to me, one day in the future, my face or your face will pop up in someone's memory and the question to ask now is, when we do pop up in their 3:00 morning experience, how will they remember us? Will whoever that person is say; we had a great time at the beach or we had hot dogs at the park or we ate candy in the movie? I'm sure they are all great memories, but I would rather their thoughts were something like, that was a man or woman of God. That guy was always helping me to understand what scripture meant or that woman was always showing me what a Christ-centered life was like and how important a smile can be to others.

Give you an example, when we think of names like Corrie-Ten- Boon or Billy Graham or Mother Teresa, I'm sure the mental image that pops up is not we had hot dogs together or we went swimming at the pool together, but more along the lines of how that person was a spiritual giant or how they loved the Lord and took others under their wings to nurture and impart spiritual insights that they themselves had lived.

Don't get me wrong, there's nothing wrong with the memories that include hot dogs, popcorn and warm breezes in the back of a convertible in the spring with your friends, but as long as we are alive, we need to let the main thing be the main thing and Jesus has to be the main thing. So the question becomes what will your legacy be when you are gone? What will you be remembered for or what difference are you making in the life of those around you today?

If you are a frequent listener of the Tea Table, you probably already noticed that there aren't a lot of scripture quotes in today's message and I don't think there needs to be lots of scripture. I think there needs to be lots of down to earth answers to the question, what difference am I making in the lives of those around me, to my friends and family or what legacy am I leaving behind? By the way, legacy is nothing more than inheritance or birthright or treasure.

Treasure, what a strange word. It conjures up a mental image of priceless jewels or gold and silver or sunken chests filled with pearls, diamonds and rubies. Do you realize your life and what you're doing with it can be a treasure to someone else? It can literally be a life-saver. A physical life-saver, as-well-as a spiritual life-saver.

Your life can help someone get out of a rut in this physical life, maybe financially or words of hope and encouragement and your life can be used by God to bring someone into the Kingdom of Heaven. Your life can be like a trumpet on the wall to bring a person or maybe an entire family out of darkness and into the light or out of death into life.

You my friend, yes you, who are alive and listening to this Tea Table message can make a difference in the lives of others around you, you can leave more than just a great memory and good feelings in the lives of others. When can you start doing that? How about right now because you never know how soon it will be too late, either for you or for that other person that God has allowed you to cross paths with.

Remember there are no coincidences, accidents or luck in life, just God choosing to remain anonymous, which means nameless or unnamed just like in the book of Esther.

Prayer: Lord, help me neither to dwell in the past which is dead and gone nor the future that doesn't exist, but to focus on the present which is a gift, that's why it's called a present.

1. Have you ever spent so much time dwelling on what could have been that you miss the opportunity to do something special in the now?
2. Can you agree that people don't live in the past, but their past lives in their present which prevents them from having a great and Godly future? Why do you agree or disagree?

Week 28
Gifts

Ever have a teaching that although you already know it, it still ignites a desire in you to want to live it out or understand it deeper? I believe today's teaching is one of those teachings.

I had a person once ask me a question and also gave me permission to be perfectly honest in my response. They asked me, "Can I continue smoking and still go to heaven"? I answered, of course you can, and as a matter of fact you will probably get there faster". This person said, what do you mean and I gave all the negative side effects of what smoking does to the body and the positive side effects of quitting. This person said to me, I already know that. My response was, to know something and not to do something about it, is really not to know it.

Just to put your mind at ease, this is not a teaching on the effects of smoking or any of the vices that we practice. This is a teaching on knowing what you already know. This is a teaching on the awareness of the gifts that we have been given from God, whether we use them or not and I would venture to say that most of us do not use our Godly gifts nor do we even think about them until we get in to a situation that we need to remind ourselves that we have them, and still, it's just a head knowledge acknowledgement that they were given to us and in all reality, we have no idea how to utilize the many gifts that we so desperately need to incorporate into our daily lives.

What do you mean, Don? Well, first of all, we need to understand exactly what a gift is. Another word for gift is: grant or present or even endowment. In other words, it's something that someone else has given you and it's a permanent contribution that now belongs to you, whether you use it or not.

In **2 Thessalonians 3:16,** we are told now may the Lord of peace himself give you peace at all times in every way. The Lord be with you all. So who's the Lord of peace? He's the same as the Prince of Peace, and peace belongs to Him and He has the right to give it to anyone that He wants to give it to. As a gift, Jesus has given that peace to you and Jesus doesn't take it back. So who owns the peace of God? You do.

What exactly is peace? According to the ancient Hebrew, peace is that which destroys the authority that establishes chaos. Peace is much more than the lack of struggle, it's being whole and complete in Jesus, the one who gave us His peace. Just to be sure, we are told again in **John 14:27,** peace I leave with you; my peace I give to you. Not as the world gives do I give to you. Let not your hearts be troubled, neither let them be afraid.

So we have the peace of God and we have it at all times and do we use it at all times? No. We don't live in peace, but usually in pieces. What are we supposed to do with God's peace? Without quoting book, chapter and verse, we are in God's peace to both lie down and sleep, we are to trust, and not be afraid. I can mention dozens of verses that tell us how to act with the peace of God, but if you're not walking in it, it's just head knowledge.

Remember, to know something and not to do it is really not to know it, and that's just one gift that we have been given.

You see, my friend, the gifts of God, like the Word of God, is not to be accumulated or collected, but to be lived and utilized. Utilized, what a big word, what does it mean? It means to be applied, used and developed.

I don't want this teaching to be about the gifts of God; I want this teaching to make you aware that God has already given you good and perfect gifts and they are yours, they belong to you. We are told in **1 Peter 4:10** as each of you has received gifts. In **Ephesians 2:8-9** for by grace you have been saved through faith. And this is not your own doing; it is the gift of God. Again in **1 Timothy 4:14**, do not neglect the gift you have.

I could go on and on, but the point is God has given gifts to us and we are to use these gifts for daily living, for making decisions, for helping others in need, for drawing nearer to the giver of the gifts, to raising our families, to living a life that is not only a testimony of stability to neighbors and friends, but to reveal that our trust and hope is not in self, or finances or government or even education, but the giver of each and every perfect gift that equips us to get through the day and to do so victoriously.

We should never get to the place where our response is: I know God has healed me, but... I know God has delivered me, but... I know God can, but... What's the answer, get off your but and tell it like it is, I know God has healed me, I know God has delivered me, I know God can, blessed be the name of the Lord.

Prayer: Father, you are the giver of all good gifts, help me to appreciate the many gifts and talents you have given me and to stop comparing and complaining about what I don't have, but to be thankful for what I do have from you.

1. Do you ever look at another person and wish you could have been more like them or desire what they do and how they do it?
2. Do you ever feel like God made a big mistake when he created you because in your eyes you can't do anything right? Do you really believe God makes mistakes?

Week 29
My People Perish

I was sitting in the backyard the other day and I heard very clearly in my spirit, vision is very important, especially self-vision. We are told in **Hosea 4:6a**, my people are destroyed from lack of knowledge. Another version says 'my people are being destroyed or ruined because they don't know me.'

I remember using a phrase when speaking to people that tell me; I know that, but deep down, they really don't know what they are speaking about. I tell them; to know something and not to do it means you don't know it.

Example, sometimes I will speak to people with permission about the health problems associated with smoking. Without getting super spiritual, I explain the negative benefits that smoking causes like cancer, heart disease, premature aging, and lack of oxygen to the blood system, not to mention the smell on their clothes and breathe and cost involved. After I explain all these things, the person will tell me, I know that but still they refuse to quit or even try to quit and some have even told me, I like smoking. My response would be; to know something and not to do something about it is the same as not knowing it.

It's absolutely amazing how relevant **Hosea 4:6a** is to us today, my people are being destroyed because they don't know me, another version we often see is; my people are being destroyed because of lack of vision.

Vision of what? Of God himself. What is this actually telling us? The children of God are coming to ruin or destruction because they don't have a clear revelation, visualization or image of their heavenly Father.

If we look at that verse closely, it's telling us we, the children of the living God are being ruined, devastated or wrecked and all because we don't know God. Sure, we have an idea about God and some may know more than others but truth be told, we have all scratched just the surface of knowing God and because of that, we really don't know how to live our lives as we should.
You see my friends, if we don't know the deeper things of God, how will we know how to live our lives as the children of God? Most children get their identity from their parents and if we only have a brief glimmer of our heavenly Father, how can we understand how we are to live our lives to the fullest.

Example: in **Philippians 4:13**, we are told I am able to do all things through Him who strengthens me. Again in **Romans 3:37**, we are encouraged with; No, in all things, we are more than conquerors through him who loved us. Did you hear that? In both verses, it tells us all things, not some things or most things or important things, but all things through Him.

The question becomes if we are told that we are able to do all things through Him and we are more than conquerors in all things through him and we believe that, do our lives reflect that we are actually living our lives doing all things as more than conquerors or is it just a wonderful memory verse while we live our lives far below our God given abilities and capabilities and calling resulting in being overwhelmed because of our lack of vision of who God, our heavenly Father really is.

You see, we come back to the statement; to know God and not to do what He tells us is not to know God. You might be asking yourself how best to make that statement. Easy, because doing what He tells us to do is called obedience and blessings will always follow obedience. In **1 Kings 3:14**, we are told if you walk in obedience to me and keep my decrees and commands as David your father did, I will give you a long life." Again, in **Isaiah 1:19,** we are told If you are willing and obedient, you will eat the good things of the land…

The bottom line is, if we truly knew God and that every promise of His was really yes and amen and that He was able to do everything He says He can do, then we would do everything in our power to do as He tells us to do because the fruit of obedience are the blessings of God. The problem is since we don't truly know God as we are supposed to know God, we suffer from lack of vision, which has a negative outcome, which is we don't live the supernatural life as children of the Most High God.

You see, as children of God, we are not supposed to live our lives under the circumstances, but over the circumstances. We are not to live our lives with a spirit of fear or condemnation or the tail and not the head, these are not the position of a conqueror or a person able to do all things in Christ.

My friends this takes us back to **Hosea 4:6a**, my people are being destroyed or ruined because they don't know me, but just the opposite would be true for the people of God who do know Him and I don't mean who know of Him, they are not being destroyed or ruined but maintained, protected and saved.

What a blessing there is in knowing God. We establish a deeper level of intimacy, our walk with Him becomes more stable and we are maintained, protected and saved, but even more, we walk in the walk that God has ordained us to walk in as able to do all things through Christ, more than conquerors in Christ and the head not the tail.
My friend, if you truly want to walk in the blessings of God, I encourage you to walk in obedience to God, and the blessings will overtake you. As a matter of fact, even if you try to out-run the blessing of God, they will overtake you, and totally and completely engulf you.

Prayer: Lord, help me to have a teachable spirit and a moldable heart and to realize that you are constantly teaching me how to war in the spirit so that I don't perish from ignorance.

1. If the word of God says his people perish from lack of knowledge, what kind of knowledge do you think he is speaking about?
2. Has the Lord ever tried to teach you something from your mistakes and you put up a wall? Why do you think you would have done that?

Week 30
Go Tell it on the Mountain

The other day I was doing what I usually do and that is listen to Christmas music. I really enjoy Christmas music and it doesn't make any difference what time of the year it is. I enjoy Christmas songs in November and December as much as August and September.

So here I was sitting and enjoying the music when the song, 'Go Tell It on the Mountain' came on, and for some reason, the words jumped off the speaker to me and I knew the Lord was prompting me to do a message on what He was showing me.

As Norma and I travel around the world, we have been able to see many very large mountain ranges. We were blessed to see the Alps in Austria, the Pyrenees in Spain, the Saw Tooth mountain range in Idaho, the Rockies, and the Blue Ridge just to mention a few. One thing about mountains, they all look great from a distance, especially when their tops are covered in snow and they stand out as majestic monuments to our great creator.

From a distance, all mountains look like a piece of cake, but up close, they are bigger than life. While in Germany, a wonderful couple, and Norma and I decided to visit a restaurant for lunch on top of a mountain and the only way to get there was to walk. At first, I thought it was a great idea. An hour into the walk, I thought I was going to die. Not being in the best of shape, all I could do was try to get enough air in to my lungs and still smile at our friends who were accustom to mountain climbing.

I made a few observations on the way up the mountain. There are no escalators, no lighted path ways or shops or rest areas and worst of all, you have to walk back down the way you went up. By the time we finished our coffee and cake, it was dark out. Did I mention there are no escalators? There was no way I was walking back down that mountain in the dark. I asked one of the workers if she could drive us to our car, and thank God, she said yes.

Mountains are an impressive fortress that don't move and can represent your biggest obstacle in life. They are extremely dangerous, as can be attested by the amount of deaths on Mount Everest each and every year.

For many a mountain in your life can mean a secluded, isolated or hard to reach place. Such a place could symbolize loneliness or a difficult to achieve place. For many, our obstacles may not start out as a mountain, but as a hill and we work really hard to make it a mountain. Ever heard the expression making a mountain out of a mole hill? It's an expression that's been around since 1660 and means you are taking something small, such as a molehill, and making it out to be bigger than it actually is. This expression is typically applied to difficulties people have. Often times, people will argue or blow out of proportion the most insignificant things.

So what did the Lord show me? He showed me that since mountains symbolize problems, difficulties, hard times, obstacles, as-well-as physical, spiritual and emotional complications in our lives and that Jesus Christ came for many reasons such as: for freedom Christ has set us free; stand firm therefore, and do not submit again to a yoke of slavery or so if the Son sets you free, you will be free indeed. How about there is therefore no condemnation for those who are in Christ Jesus any longer. For those living in the shadow of the mountain called fear, we can thank God because God gave us a spirit not of fear, but of power, love and self-control.

My friends, we can, should and must go tell it on the mountain, whatever that mountain is, that Jesus Christ is born.

Why is that important? Because since Jesus Christ is born and knowing that God cannot lie and every promise of God is a yes and amen, then every mountain in our lives must bow their knees to the Lordship of Jesus Christ. Fear must bow its knee, sickness and illness must bow its knee, slavery to our thoughts and desires must bow its knee and addiction must bow its knee because we are told by He who cannot lie that one day every knee shall bow to the Lordship of Jesus Christ.

In other words, we proclaim and declare: mountain of fear, Jesus Christ is born to take away my fear and replace it with love, power and a sound mind. Mountain of sickness, Jesus Christ is born and by His stripes I am healed.

Whatever your mountain is in life, Jesus Christ is born and because of that you can tell that mountain to be cast into the sea and that, my friend, is freedom and what we have been called to walk in and all because Jesus Christ is born, you and I will boldly go tell that on the mountain.

Prayer: Precious heavenly Father, help me to realize that just because something looks like an obstacle or a mountain in my life, doesn't mean it looks the same way to you. Teach me how to depend more on you and less on myself to overcome the mountains of life.

1. When you are confronted with a mountain in your life, do you try to avoid it, go around it, sneak under it or ask God to overcome it in his strength?
2. What are examples of mountains in your life? What do you do with them?

Week 31
Hang on to the Promise

Do you remember when you were a kid or even an adult for that matter and someone promised you something and your expectations were aroused for the fulfillment of that promise, but somehow, the ball was dropped and the promise was forgotten. Do you remember how you felt, that let down feeling? You were really anticipating the promise they made to you to actually be carried out.

Depending on the seriousness of the promise, the feeling of being let down was either a no big deal, don't worry about it or my God, how could they have forgotten that, it was really, really important to me.

Give you an example, in **2 Kings 20,** we are told: in those days Hezekiah became ill and was at the point of death. The prophet Isaiah son of Amos went to him and said, "This is what the Lord says: Put your house in order, because you are going to die; you will not recover." Hezekiah turned his face to the wall and prayed to the Lord, "Remember, Lord, how I have walked before you faithfully and with wholehearted devotion and have done what is good in your eyes." And Hezekiah wept bitterly. Before Isaiah had left the middle court, the word of the Lord came to him: "Go back and tell Hezekiah, the ruler of my people, 'This is what the Lord, the God of your father David, says: I have heard your prayer and seen your tears; I will heal you. On the third day from now you will go up to the temple of the Lord. I will add fifteen years to your life. And I will deliver you and this city from the hand of the king of Assyria. I will defend this city for my sake and for the sake of my servant David.' "

Talk about an amazing promise, one moment ago, Hezekiah had a death sentence over his head and one moment latter, Hezekiah had 15 more years added to his life.

Who was Isaiah? Granted, he was a prophet of God, but he was just a human, just a person like many of us. The question becomes where will I put my eyes? On the man who gave the promise or the promise of God that came through the Man. If you put your eyes on the man, you have a real problem because man will always disappoint you and let you down, but if your eyes are on God, He will never disappoint you or let you down.

If you are anything like me, when I pray for a person, there are two major things that I need to remember, one, I can't save anyone and two, I can't heal anyone. That, my friend, takes a big weight off my shoulders because it has to be God, which brings me back to the title of this message; hang on to the promise.

If God has given you a promise, any promise, a spouse or help mate, a child anything, a healing, don't look to the person who gave you the word, look to the Giver of all good gifts, your heavenly Father who tells us He is not a man that He should lie and that all of His promises to you are Yes.

I'll give you a really solid example. In three days, I will be going for open heart surgery. The enemy has been trying to have a field day with me with everything that can go wrong, but last year, a brother in the Lord had a word for me. He told me the Lord said I will give you Don, 10 more years of ministry and if you want another 10 years after that, just ask and I will give you 10 more years. Are my eyes on the brother that brought forth the word? Absolutely not, they are on the Lord and I believe the word that said; 10 more years of life are from God and I am literally betting my very life on that.

There is nothing more disappointing than arriving at the parade only to find the parade has already passed you by. There are many promises we have had from people that came and went, but the fulfillment of the promise has passed you by because the giver of the promise either got busy or was just giving you lip service or was telling you something that they thought you wanted to hear.

When God gives you a promise, you can bet the farm that He will fulfill the promise. When Jesus promised us that He will never leave us nor forsake us, He means what He says and says what He means and regardless of whatever you are going through, He is there with us, going through the same thing. We are told in **Deuteronomy 31:8**, "The LORD himself goes before you and will be with you; he will never leave you nor forsake you. Do not be afraid; do not be discouraged."

My friends, there are literally dozens of times in scripture where God tells us that He will be there with us. We may feel lonely, but we are never alone.

You see with man, they may make a promise and really intend to keep the promise, but there are so many obstacles to keeping the promise. They may not have the ability to keep their promise or they may not have the strength or finances or know-how, but with God, He tells us in **Mark 10:27,** Jesus looked at them intently and said, "Humanly speaking, it is impossible. But not with God. Everything is possible with God." Again in **Matthew 19:26,** we are told But Jesus looked at them and said, "With man, this is impossible, but with God, all things are possible."

If God has made you a promise, which He has and if a word was given to you through a brother or sister, my advice is to hang onto that promise, never let it go, there is a cord that binds you to the very promise that God made and its called faith. The cord-of-faith looks like this: God, I believe the promise you made to me. I don't understand it, I can't see it, I don't know how it will come to pass, but I believe it and I will hang on to it the best way I can with the strength that I have.

There are many out there that God said He will give you a help mate, He will give you a child, He will heal you or use doctors to bring about your healing, He said He will deliver you from that court case, or He will save your husband or wife or son or daughter or He will deliver someone you know from drugs or alcohol or that over-eating disorder that is killing you. Regardless of how difficult or impossible the promise is, God is more than willing and more than able to do it, just as we are told in Mark 1:40, and a leper came to Jesus, beseeching Him and falling on his knees before Him, and saying, "If You are willing, You can make me clean." Moved with compassion, Jesus stretched out His hand and touched him, and said to him, "I am willing; be cleansed.

My friends, Jesus is willing and Jesus is able, be healed, be delivered, be complete, be at peace in the promise of God for your life, your family, your business, your marriage and your health.

Prayer: Lord, teach me to understand that all the promises you have given me for my life are yes and amen regardless of the fact that I don't see them coming to pass in my life.

1. Do you sometimes feel like God has forgotten a promise he made to you about your life because it seems so very far away?
2. Do you really believe that God is not a man that he should lie or does it just too good to be true? Do you sometimes judge God based on your life experiences?

Week 32
What's the Magic Word?

Do you remember when you were a little kid and you really wanted something, and so, you asked one of the adults around you; 'gimme me that toy' only to hear 'what's the magic word'? So again, you asked; I want that toy or candy or whatever it was. And again you would hear 'what's the magic word'? Finally, after what seemed like an eternity you said 'please' and received that which you wanted.

As a child with a limited vocabulary, it was hard to figure out how a little word, like please, could open up so many wonderful opportunities for us. As we got older, the word please became easier to use with wonderful results and so eventually, that magic word became part of our daily vocabulary.

I've discovered that as we grow older, there are many magic words that bring wonderful results into our lives and so I would like to cover just a few of the magic words that need to be spoken often and daily so they become part of our vocabulary.

There are the magic words I Love You. These words can be spoken to children, spouse, and friends, and even to the Lord. The good thing about the expression, I Love You, is that there is no expiration date or quota or geographical limitation to them. You can use those three little words anytime you want and as many times you like and wherever you want to use them. If they are three little words that you have a hard time saying, you can even practice using them by looking in to the mirror and telling yourself that you love yourself and by the way, I'm not speaking about self-love, but Godly love because you are the reflection of God himself.

We are told in **James 3:9** "With the tongue we praise our Lord and Father, and with it, we curse human beings, who have been made in God's likeness." Again in **Genesis 1:27,** "So, God created mankind in his own image, in the image of God he created them; male and female he created them."

1 Corinthians 11:7 "A man, in fact, should not cover his head, because he is God's image and glory, but woman is man's glory."

If God can love that which He has created, I believe we can love that which He has created also, and that means each other, as-well-as ourselves.

This is for the guys out there; I can remember Norma asking me if I love her to which I said, of course I do. She said you need to tell me that more often. I said 'I show you my love in many other ways like cooking, helping you with chores etc.' I don't need to keep on telling you I love you.' I made a discovery, guys, yes, you do! You need to keep on telling your wives and your children that you love them and appreciate them. Remember, hearing the expression, I'm not a mind-reader, how would I know if you don't tell me?

I love you, is a wonderful magic word that can truly open many doors, and at the same time, bring great joy and comfort to others around you. One more thing, the words I Love You, must come from a sincere heart and not just an empty expression to get that which you want.

There's another magic word out there that is very amazing, and when used from a sincere heart, can bring the most miraculous results not only to others, but to us as well. That word is, I forgive you. I can remember thinking, that to forgive was to forget. How wrong I was. To forgive is to remember, but choose not to hold resentment or cease to blame the person that wronged against me. Sometimes, one of the most difficult things to do is to respond to a hurt done against us by showing kindness.

I'm learning that true forgiveness is a three way action. First, I ask my Heavenly Father to forgive me, I ask the person to whom the hurt came from to forgive me, and finally, and sometimes the most difficult, I forgive myself. The reason forgiving oneself is the most difficult is because the enemy will always try to remind you of what was done. But since we all know that the enemy is a liar, we can just ignore him and press in to the blessings of forgiveness.

By the way, forgiveness is more than just a good idea, it's a scriptural practice that God himself mentions often in His word with blessings and curses for forgiving and for not forgiving.

We are told in **Ephesians 4:32,** "And be kind to one another, tenderhearted, forgiving one another, even as God for Christ's sake has forgiven you." In **Mark 11:25,** "And when you stand praying, forgive, if you have anything against any: that your Father also which is in heaven may forgive you your trespasses." A really big verse is in **1 John 1:9** "If we confess our sins, he is faithful and just to forgive us our sins, and to cleanse us from all unrighteousness."

If God can forgive us for all that we have done against Him, how much more should we forgive others that have trespassed against us. Besides, forgiving is removing a heavy weight that hangs around our necks and weighs us down and binds us to the person in a negative sense. Another magic word is thank you. The word, thank you, means much more than just an appreciation or gratitude of someone's kindness.

As we were growing up, how many times have we heard the expression after something kind was done to us or for us, 'what do you say'? To which we mechanically said; thank you. Even at an early age, we were taught the value of gratitude, which means appreciation or thankfulness. It showed us not to take the kind actions of another for granted.

Giving thanks from a thankful, joyful heart is another word that was practiced and given high regards to in scripture. In **Colossians 3:17,** we are told and whatever you do, whether in word or deed, do it all in the name of the Lord Jesus, giving thanks to God the Father through him. **Ephesians 5:20,** "Always giving thanks to God the Father for everything, in the name of our Lord Jesus Christ." We are

also encouraged in **Colossians 3:15,** "Let the peace of Christ rule in your hearts, since as members of one body you were called to peace. And be thankful."
Jesus Himself said in **John 11:41** "Father, I thank you that you have heard me." In **Daniel 2:23,** Daniel says "I thank you, and praise you, O God of my fathers." In **Psalms 67:3,** we are told; "Let the people thank you, God. Let all the people thank you. ... Let the nation's thank you, O God! Let all the nations' thank you!"

If all the nations can be thankful, all the people can be thankful, Daniel can be thankful, and Jesus Himself can be thankful, how much more should we have those magic words in our vocabulary and be thankful for everything and to everyone all the time. Besides, thank you tells the other person that I'm not taking you or what you did for granted. That other person can be family, friends, spouse, co-workers or God Himself or His precious Son that we all owe a great debt of thanks to and finally to the Ruach HaKodesh the spirit or breath of God, also known as the Holy Spirit in our lives which does a work in our hearts, confirms our inheritance as God's children, reveals and teaches us about the things God has given us, reveals the truth and guides us in living a life of righteousness and those are just a few things that we can be thankful for.

Prayer: Father, help me to cherish each and every word that you speak to me either in my spirit or through your word because I know they are a light to my path and protection for my life.

1. Do you believe God is more interested in our grammatical approach to him or does he look at the heart? Why do you feel that way?
2. As a child of God, do you sometimes find yourself begging God for things or do you come into his presence with a bold confidence? What are the rights of the children of God when approaching his throne?

Week 33
The Name Above All Names

When I was in the Air Force so many years ago, I had numerous opportunities to learn valuable lessons and one of the more important lessons was you should never treat a high ranking officer the same way you treat an enlisted personnel. Example; you don't treat an airman the same way you treat a lieutenant and you don't treat a captain the same way you treat or even acted around a general and I had many occasions to come in contact with all of them often seeing that my job description was working on the flight line with pilots.

You see rank has its privileges. Three stripes is over one stripe and one gold bar is over six stripes and one star is over a gold leaf. For those who are or were in the military, you know what I'm talking about. As strange as it may seem, the ranking has absolutely nothing to do with the character of the person. You could have two stars on your collar and be the nicest guy in the world, and the ones I met usually were or you could have three stripes on your sleeve and be a real jerk. The pecking order, so to speak, had nothing to do with your personality, but your ranking or how far above you were in the chain of command.

So one more time, a major is above a captain and a lieutenant is above a sergeant and so on. It got so typical that a rank became almost identical to a name and so it was that one name above another name.

Which brings me to the heart of the message.

Do you realize that most things in life boil down to a name or what a name represents? And for all practical purposes, every name conjurers up an image. Example, if I call out the name Chevy, for some, it will evoke the image of a corvette, for others, maybe a station wagon and for others, maybe a pick-up truck and all because of a name. Another example would be if I used the name of a very evil person. For some, it may evoke the name of Hitler or any dictator, for others, maybe someone who really hurt you in your childhood or hurt your family somehow. Maybe you went to the doctor's office because you weren't feeling well and you had to undergo a series of tests and the doctor calls you in the middle of the night and says I have some bad news. Immediately, your mind brings to your attention many names such as cancer, heart disease, diabetes or whichever name may have been familiar in your family.

The point is, it's just a name, nothing more and nothing less. Do you realize that a name cannot harm you no more than a shadow can harm you? What the name represents is a different story and that's what evokes an image in our mind.

Cancer for example is just a name which evokes an image of fear which is just another name that evokes a mental image of death or dying.

Not only can't a name hurt you or harm you, but it isn't the end of your story either. You've heard the expression it isn't over until it's over. That is a very true statement because a name doesn't define when something is over. It's over when God says it's over. We read an example of that in **2 Kings 20:1-5**. In those days, Hezekiah became ill and was at the point of death. The prophet Isaiah, son of Amoz, went to him and said, "This is what the Lord says: Put your house in order, because you are going to die; you will not recover." Hezekiah turned his face to the wall and prayed to the Lord, "Remember, Lord, how I have walked before you faithfully and with wholehearted devotion and have done what is good in your eyes." And Hezekiah wept bitterly. Before Isaiah had left the middle court, the word of the Lord came to him: "Go back and tell Hezekiah, the ruler of my people, 'this is what the Lord, the God of your father David, says: I have heard your prayer and seen your tears; I will heal you.' "

A good question to ask is why Hezekiah's death sentence was over-ruled? Sure, he wept bitterly before the Lord, but I'm sure if weeping was the solution to all the death sentences out there, there would be a lot more weeping. The answer is, it's not over until God says it's over.

You see my friends, the same way that rank has its privileges because one rank is above another rank and the lower ranks have to submit and do as they are told, so do the names that evoke fear have to submit to the name above all names.

Thank God we are told, "Therefore, God has highly exalted him and bestowed on him the name that is above every name," **Philippians 2:9**. And to further add hope to our lives, we read in **Philippians 2:10** "That at the name of

Jesus, every knee should bow, in heaven and on earth and under the earth."

My friend, cancer is just a name, heart disease is just a name, poverty is just a name, drug addiction is just a name, and unemployment, as well, is just a name. Whatever situation you are in that evokes fear or failure or hopelessness in your life or your family, remember it's just a name, but there is another name that is above every name. Not only that, whichever name is trying to bring you under fear, that name has to bow its knee to the name which is above all other names and that is the name of Jesus.

What does that mean? It means that cancer has to bow its knee to the name of Jesus because Jesus is above sickness, Jesus is above heart disease, Jesus is above poverty, Jesus is above every name that is named. Not only that, my friend, but at the name of Jesus, every knee should bow, in heaven and on earth and under the earth. There is no other authority, no other power, no other anything that is above the name of Jesus. Sickness does not define your future, poverty does not define your future, and failure does not define your future because God has already defined your future when He said for I know the plans I have for you," declares the Lord, "plans to prosper you and not to harm you, plans to give you hope and a future." **Jeremiah 29:11**. In the face of a fearful name, we need to speak to our spirit and tell ourselves what is spoken in **Psalm 112:7**, he is not afraid of bad news; his heart is firm, trusting in the Lord.

Prayer: Gracious, heavenly Father, help me to understand that I can either believe what's behind a name like cancer or failure or I can believe in the name above all names, it all boils down to Whose Report will I Believe?

1. In light of **Psalm 112:7**, are you sometimes afraid of bad news or the possibility that something may be wrong?
2. When things don't go the way you want them to go, where do you usually run to or trust in? Do you really believe that God has not given you a spirit of fear?
3. If God says He has not given you a spirit of fear and you experience fear, where do you think that fear came from? What can you do about it?

Week 34
Indelibly Written

You know, there are many times I speak with young believers concerning the issue of salvation, and you won't believe the thoughts that come out of our conversations.

Some tell me; yes, I'm saved, but I don't have to change my old life style and I can continue doing everything that I use to do and not have to worry about it because I'm saved. About that time I mention, you will know them by their fruits and that will either cause an argument or a deeper discussion.

Others have said to me, I'm saved as long as I feel saved. If I feel good about myself, then, I know that I'm saved and if I do something wrong and it doesn't bother me, then I'm still saved, but if I do something wrong and feel bad about what I've done, all I have to do is ask for forgiveness and I'm saved again. Of course about this time I shift the conversation to we don't live by feelings and this brings about an argument or a deeper discussion.

The believers that are the most difficult to deal with are the ones who tell me; it's possible to lose your salvation. I ask them about their names being written in the Lamb's Book of Life and also ask them what that means. They tell me that they have accepted Jesus Christ as their Lord and Savior and they are washed in the Blood of the Lamb and they have their names written in the Lamb's Book of Life but when they sin, they lose their salvation.

About that time I ask them; how exactly does God do that? Do you think God writes their name in the Book of Life with a pencil that has an eraser at the other end, and their name is written in pencil?

If what you believe is true, imagine how busy God must be. You accept Jesus as your Savior, God writes your name in the Book of Life with a pencil and you start out as we all do, on a good and positive step. Not too long after that, you screw up and sin and God gets out the eraser and erases your name from the Book, but you claim **1 John 1:9,** if we confess our sins, he is faithful and just to forgive us our sins and to cleanse us from all unrighteousness. That word, forgive means; liberate and pardon. So God now writes your name in the Book of Life again or at least until you sin again, and let's be real, that may be in the next 10 minutes, either in thought or in deed, and God quickly comes running with His eraser and out you go from the book, at least until you claim **1 John 1:9** all over again, and back in you go.

Now, according to statistics, there are between 90-100 million evangelicals just in the United States, although Christians in America are decreasing in number every year, but regardless of that fact, knowing that we all sin, and following the belief that when you sin, you lose your salvation until you claim **1 John 1:9** and you get your name written back in the Book of Life, that would mean in America alone there would probably be billions of sins daily. God must really be busy erasing and re-writing names all day long. Does that seem to make sense to anyone? If it does, then your life must be one which is walked out on egg shells because you never know when you committed a sin and never know if and when your name has been erased. That, my friend, makes for a very uncomfortable walk through life. Why? Because your life will be one not walked out from a motive of love, but a form of legalism and fear. Granted, we are to fear the Lord, but that fear is not dread, gloom and anxiety, but awe and reverence for a loving, merciful and compassionate heavenly Father.

Besides, if your walk with God is a legalistic walk out of fear of making a mistake and sinning, then you treat God as a policeman who is waiting for you to screw up so he can whack you with His heavenly club of correction. How can you love someone that acts as a tyrant in your life waiting for you to step out of line to correct you?

Remember when you were a kid and you picked up a daisy and one by one you plucked off a pedal and said, he loves me, he loves me not, he loves me, he loves me not until all the pedals were gone and you had no idea how the ending would play out, you hoped you ended up with he loves me, but your weren't absolutely sure. Can you imagine your life with; God loves me, God loves me not, God loves me, God loves me not. That is no way to live a life that is supposed to be filled with the love of God.

My friends, if you believe you can lose your salvation, then that is exactly how you are living your life. He loves me not, **1 John 1:9**, He loves me, He loves me not, **1 John 1:9**, He loves me. It just doesn't fit, it's like putting a square peg in a round hole, and you can't even force it to make it seem right.

Here's the good news: when you accepted Christ as your Lord and Savior and your name was written in the Lamb's Book of Life, it was indelibly inscribed in that book. Just for clarification, indelibly means; permanently, forever and lastingly. Inscribed means; engraved, adorned and carved. Your name was permanently engraved, forever adorned and lastingly carved in the Book of Life. When you pluck that daisy and start to pick at the pedals, it goes something like this: He loves me, He loves me, He loves me and when you get to that place when all the pedals are gone, He still loves you and your name is still in the Book.

I was asked this question: Can you prove what you say in the Bible? And the answer is of course, because it deals with the love of God, forgiveness and repentance.

God's love is revealed in:

John 3:16, "For God so loved the world, that he gave his only Son, that whoever believes in him should not perish but have eternal life."

Romans 5:8, "But God shows his love for us in that while we were still sinners, Christ died for us."

1 John 3:1, "See what kind of love the Father has given to us, that we should be called children of God; and so we are."

Zephaniah 3:17, "The LORD your God is in your midst, a mighty one who will save; he will rejoice over you with gladness; he will quiet you by his love; he will exult over you with loud singing."

God's forgiveness is shown in:

Matthew 26:28, "For this is my blood of the covenant, which is poured out for many for the forgiveness of sins."

Isaiah 43:25, "I, even I, am he who blots out your transgressions, for my own sake, and remembers your sins no more."

Isaiah 1:18, "Come now, let us settle the matter, says the LORD. Though your sins are like scarlet, they shall be as white as snow; though they are red as crimson, they shall be like wool."

Ephesians 1:7, "In him we have redemption through his blood, the forgiveness of sins, in accordance with the riches of God's grace."

What does God says about repentance?

Isaiah 30:15, this is what the Sovereign LORD, the Holy One of Israel, says: "In repentance and rest is your salvation, in quietness and trust is your strength, but you would have none of it.

Acts 3:19, "Repent, then, and turn to God, so that your sins may be wiped out, that times of refreshing may come from the Lord,"

Romans 2:4, "Or do you show contempt for the riches of his kindness, forbearance and patience, not realizing that God's kindness is intended to lead you to repentance?"

So my friends, when you do sin, realize that you do not lose your salvation but because of God's great love towards us, he allows us to repent of our sins, He forgives us of our sins and we press on to the great calling that He has for our lives, and to that, I say thank you Lord for your great love.

Prayer: Father, you have so many promises about my life, help me to realize that every promise is absolutely true regardless of what I think or feel and to know each promise is written down in your book of my life.

1. God has so many promises for your life; do you have difficulties laying ahold of them in your life? Why do you think that is?
2. What is it that keeps you from believing they are true for you?
3. Do you sometimes believe God's promises for others more than God's promises for yourself?

Week 35
Titles

Isn't it amazing how and where God speaks to us? I was in church today and right in the middle of praise and worship, I heard a familiar voice say: teach on titles. The song we were singing had nothing to do with the subject titles and I had no idea what I was to speak about, so I asked the Lord to remind me of an incident that had something to do with titles. Thank God His memory is much better than mine.

The Lord brought me back to an incident that happened many years ago. So many years ago that I had completely and totally forgot about the incident. I was in a job where a position had opened and I applied for the position. I was pretty sure I was going to get the position because there was no question that I was the most qualified. I even told myself that there was no way that I couldn't get the title and the position that I had applied for.

A short period of time went by and amazing, absolutely amazing, someone else got the position. Talk about being really upset. I went before the Lord and said: Lord, what gives? I'm the most qualified; the best candidate for the position and the other person that got the job is the least qualified. I mean, I have a B.A., and a B.S., and an MBA, which means I deserve the title of the job and the position, after all, I'm the only one out of all those who applied for the job that deserves it and is most qualified for the position.

Needless to say, I wasn't in much of a mood to carry on a conversation with anyone for a few days because I was going on and on in my mind about how I was the only qualified one and it should have been mine. Now, I'm well aware that in the presence of the Lord, the mountains melt beneath him and the valleys split apart, like wax before the fire, like water rushing down a slope.

As I think back on the entire incident, it's hard for me to believe that I was carrying on so much about a title until the Lord spoke and like **Job 38:2, 3**. I heard: "Who is this that complicates or muddles my plans with words without knowledge? Brace yourself like a man; I will question you, and you shall answer me."

He said to me; 'son, I know your titles and degrees, but did you know that I have a few titles also? Did you know that I am the Alpha and the Omega, I am the first and the last, I am the King of Kings and the Lord of Lords? I'm also the Lion of the Tribe of Judah and The First-born from the dead. As a matter of fact son, I have over 900 titles of not only who I am, but what I do and I believe that qualifies Me to be your God and your Lord and I don't carry on as much as you do when you give one of my titles to something or someone else.'

Like **Job in 40:4, 5**. My only position was: "I am unworthy—how can I reply to you? I put my hand over my mouth. I spoke once, but I have no answer—twice, but I will say no more."

162

The Lord reminded me that King David, His faithful servant had enough sense to strip off his priestly robes in the presence of God Almighty. He also showed me that David, the greatest king that ever lived was not into titles, but into the presence of God. When you strip off your priestly robes, you are stripping off your many titles before God. What titles did King David have, you might be asking? David was Prince over Israel, he was King over Judah and King over Israel, and that, my friend, is a King over a population of 5,000,000 plus people.

So really, what titles do we have or own that have not been given to us from God? What have we accomplished that God has not been directing our footsteps through life. Really, ask yourself what great accomplishment or triumph or success in life have we obtained that God was not there leading us in to victory. Maybe you accumulated great wealth, I'm told you shall remember the Lord your God, for it is he who gives you power to get wealth, **Deuteronomy 8:18**. Maybe you're very intelligent and full of wisdom, don't get puffed up, remember; for the Lord gives wisdom; from his mouth come knowledge and understanding **Proverbs 2:6**. Maybe you're a really great student, always on the Dean's list. Your ability to learn didn't just happen, like the young Hebrew boys in Daniel we are told, as for these four youths, God gave them learning and skill in all literature and wisdom.

I think you see where I'm going; these are just things, titles like diplomas and job descriptions, wealth and intelligence. None of us are entitled to any of these things; nothing is owed us because of what we did in our own strength.

Why? Because it's not your strength, the Lord is your strength and He gives strength to His people, it's His strength and He gave it to us.

Truth be told, the only thing we can do without the Lord is fail, but with the Lord as **Philippians 4:13** tells us, "I can do all things through him who strengthens me." Even your victories in life don't belong to you because of your great abilities. **Deuteronomy 20:4** tells us "For the Lord your God is he who goes with you to fight for you against your enemies, to give you the victory."

Tell me, what could you possibly boast about while standing in the presence of God Almighty? What list of titles or diplomas or accomplishments or bank accounts could you show Him that He would be impressed with? There is nothing we can do or learn or accomplish that will win us any special favor with the Most High.

As He once told me, 'son, I've seen you at your very best and I really wasn't that impressed.' Truly, everything we have, we got from God, but don't think for a second that God gave you everything that He has, God has a lot more to give you.

What does God want from us? To strip away our priestly robes, lay aside our titles and diplomas and accomplishments, and love Him with all our heart, soul, mind and strength and worship Him and only Him for who He is and not what He does. In other words, look into His eyes not at His hands, after all, a good Father gives good gifts to His children as we are told every good and perfect gift is from above, coming down from the Father of the heavenly lights, who does not change like shifting shadows **James 1:17**.

Everything we have that has come from our heavenly Father is not only good, but perfect as well and He loves to shower us with gifts as any parent would do for a loving child. My friends, we don't need manmade titles or self-proclaimed accomplishments or do it yourself victories when we have been blessed with all the blessings in the heaven and they come from a loving, gracious, compassionate heavenly Father that loves us beyond words.

Prayer: Heavenly Father, give me understanding that with all the gifts and accomplishments and titles that I have, that they were because of you in my life and they mean nothing when compared with who you are.

1. What could you possibly boast about while standing in the presence of God Almighty?
2. What list of titles or diplomas or accomplishments or bank accounts could you show God that He would be impressed with?
3. What is it that you have that God has not supplied you with? Where did they come from?

Week 36
Closure

The Lord woke me up at 5:30 in the morning with the word closure. Not a message or a sermon or a story, but just a word, closure. Having done this so many times, I almost automatically knew what had to be done. Notice I said what had to be done and not would have liked to have been done. I would have liked to roll over and go back to sleep for a few more hours, but what had to be done was get up and sit in front of my laptop and wait and see what the Lord had for me to write about.

Now, I know closure means; finish, termination, end or conclusion, but that's just a definition of the word and not necessarily the definition of an actual situation in someone's life.

How many times as a youngster have you asked your Mom for something and she says NO! Sooo you asked again and got the same response, Noooo. Two minutes later, yep, you asked again, only louder and you kept this up until you pushed the right buttons and finally after 8 or 9 tries, got a yes or okay or if I do this, will you stop bothering me?

You would have thought the first NO would have brought closure or by definition, a termination or conclusion to the asking, but you see my friends, closure is not always closure and it doesn't always mean it's the end to a situation.

As a young man or woman dating, how many times have you tried to sneak in a little kiss at the end of a date and the other person said no? So being persistent, you kept trying, and after so many attempts, finally got that little good night kiss. By definition, the first No should have brought closure or an end to the trying, but as I mentioned, closure is not always closure.

Maybe the new job didn't pan out the way you thought it was going to go or the finances are not where they need to be, or the relationship seems to really be on the rocks, or maybe a worst case scenario. Maybe the x-rays or tests came back from the doctor and the report is not what you wanted to hear. Maybe you heard; there's nothing more to be done, its terminal and the enemy whispers in your ear, this is closure, the end, it's over. My friends, closure doesn't mean it's over.

Don, how can you say that? This is a doctor, an authority on this death sentence. Let's be real, a doctor is just a doctor, and being human, they make mistakes. We have all heard of cases that were misdiagnosed or surgeries on the wrong area of the body. And again, I don't care who the person is that brings the bad news, it's not over until the Lord says it's over and even then, listen to me, even then, it doesn't mean it's over.

Kind of reminds me of the story of Hezekiah in **2 Kings 20:1-6**. In those days Hezekiah became ill and was at the point of death. The prophet Isaiah son of Amos went to him and said, "This is what the Lord says: Put your house in order, because you are going to die; you will not recover." Hezekiah turned his face to the wall and prayed to the Lord, "Remember, Lord, how I have walked before you faithfully and with wholehearted devotion and have done what is good in your eyes." And Hezekiah wept bitterly. Before Isaiah had left the middle court, the word of the Lord came to him: "Go back and tell Hezekiah, the ruler of my people, 'this is what the Lord, the God of your father David, says: I have heard your prayer and seen your tears; I will heal you. On the third day from now you will go up to the temple of the Lord. I will add fifteen years to your life.' "

This just wasn't a no-body, this was Isaiah, a prophet of the Lord, someone who heard the voice of God, knew what God's voice sounded like and one who was obedient to say exactly what the Lord had told him to say. I mean if there was a situation where closure seemed like it was really a final decision, it was when this prophet of God says: "This is what the Lord says: Put your house in order, because you are going to die; you will not recover."

Man, if I heard that, I would have thought it doesn't get any more closure oriented than that. That is as I've heard, signed, sealed and delivered, go directly to jail and do not pass go. It my mind, those words would have been the final curtain. And my friends, with that kind of thinking, I would have been completely wrong.

Think about it. If you were given a death sentence by a doctor and you asked someone to pray for you, what would you be expecting? That person to say to you, get your things in order, it's over and done for you or would you

168

want a person filled with hope and anticipation that God is still more than able to turn this thing around completely and totally.

Personally, I don't want people who want to carry my casket high, I want people to lift my Spirits high with hope and can do and believing that with God all things are possible. In other words, with God, even the impossible is possible. As Corrie ten Boom said, never be afraid to trust an unknown future to a known God."

What were the actions that seemingly changed God's mind? We read that Hezekiah prayed to the Lord and Hezekiah wept bitterly before the Lord.

In situations where everything seems to be out of control and your whole world is falling apart, what do you do? I have never read where getting mad and losing control solved anything. Prayer and weeping before the Lord has always been a great winning combination. We are told, therefore I tell you, whatever you ask in prayer, believe that you have received it, and it will be yours **Mark 11:24**. Pray without ceasing **1 Thessalonians 5:17**.

We are also encouraged, but when you pray, go into your room and shut the door and pray to your Father who is in secret. And your Father who sees in secret will reward you. **Matthew 6:6.**

I've also learned that weeping is a great way to get God's attention. And please, don't tell me; real men don't cry. We are told in **John 11:35** Jesus wept. And David went up the ascent of the Mount of Olives, and wept as he went, and his head was covered and he walked barefoot. Then all the people who were with him each covered his head and went up weeping as they went, **2 Samuel 15:30**. So the people came to Bethel and sat there before God until evening, and lifted up their voices and wept bitterly, **Judges 21:2**.

What is weeping if not expressing grief, sorrow, or any overwhelming emotion by shedding tears? God is our heavenly Father, and as a Father, He is very much concerned with His children's grief or sorrow or any overwhelming emotion and when you are experiencing that, the natural thing to do is to speak to the one you love and share your feelings, and that, my friend, is prayer, talking to the one who really understands what you are going through and in this case, God, the only one who really understands, and can truly make a difference; by truly making a difference, for with man, it is impossible, but with God all things are possible.

Prayer: Lord, I know you don't change your mind when it comes to the important things in my life, so help me to not to be wishy washy with your word, but to believe that when I give you all the choices, you make the very best decision for me.

1. Do you sometimes think that yelling and complaining will get God to relent on what he's asked you to do? Justify your answer.
2. Do you think that some of the things that God has asked you to do are way beyond your ability?

3. Why do you believe that God would ask you to do something that he knows you can't do? Why did you answer the way you did?

Week 37
Paid in Full, Null and Void

The other day I was driving with Norma and the Lord planted a seed in my mind. Out of the clear, a thought came to me accompanied by a vision. I saw a farmer take a seed and drop it in a hole in the ground. It was the same way the Lord dropped this very seed in my mind which was the basis for today's message. I heard very clearly; paid in full, null and void. As I thought about this expression that my faithful heavenly Father gave me, I began to think of the words and how they applied to my life and it brought back some great memories.

I remember many years ago while living in Puerto Rico, Norma and I accompanied a dear brother to an art dealership because he wanted to have something framed. We were on the other side of this very large store, looking at a selection of art work when we came across an artist that we both liked very much. I remember mentioning to Norma that I really liked this particular painting and she agreed. Mind you, we were completely alone and speaking to each other very low about something we were looking at in an art album. My brother was done so we left and went back home. A few weeks later, we get a call from this art dealership and he tells me, the picture has come in and it's ready for pick up. I tell him I didn't order a painting. We go back and forth for about 15 minutes, so I decided to go in to the store and settle this once and for all. I get there and they show me the exact painting that Norma and I said we liked very much. I told him we didn't order the painting and couldn't afford it anyway. To which we are told, it's yours and it has been paid in full. Twice, I reassure him that I didn't buy it and I asked my dear brother that we went with and he said he didn't buy it nor could he afford it. I said to the man, it's paid in full? Yes he replied, so I said, wrap it up, I'm taking it home. To this day, we have a wonderful gift that we have no idea who heard us and who paid for it, but I have a sneaking suspicion the one who gave us this wonderful gift and paid for it has his residency in heaven. Paid in full, what a wonderful sound.

Every once in a while, Norma and I will go to a restaurant to enjoy a meal and we ask the Lord which table would you like us to pay for their meal and He always points out a table. I call the waiter over and ask him to bring me the bill for that other table, and we pay their bill in full. We never hang around, but we enjoy thinking about the reaction when they ask for their bill and the waiter tells them, your bill has been paid in full. Not only is it great fun for us and surprise for the other table, but even the waiter or waitress gets caught up in what we're doing, we had one waiter tell us, this is the coolest thing ever, and he had to tell the other staff members what we did. Paid in full, what a wonderful expression of release.

There's another word that can bring joy if used correctly and that's the word void which also means; cancelled or annulled. I remember after my open heart surgery, we were waiting for a bill from the doctor and the hospital that would have been astronomical. We waited and waited and after some time came to the realization that whatever the

173

amount was, it had been paid in full and the bill was null and void. Thank you Lord.

The last word that can bring joy is null, which also means; insignificant, unimportant and unacceptable. I remember quite a while ago having a situation that involved the judicial system and of no fault of mine, I was involved in a case that was pending against me where the other person wanted to throw me under the truck. Serious prayer went up, and after many months, the decision came down from the Supreme Court that the case against me was insignificant and actions taken against me were unacceptable and it was thrown out of the court system. Again, thank you Lord.

Were all three of these examples just coincidence of things going on in my life? Of course not. We are told the steps of a man are established by the Lord **Psalm 37:23**. Sometimes, my friend, God has to direct your steps to where He wants to bless you just like He directed our steps to an art dealership so He could bless us with a painting that we didn't even know existed. When God directs our footsteps, it also means we have a mission or task to walk out the steps or the plans that are being directed by God for our lives and God has wonderful plans for us. For I know the plans I have for you, declares the Lord, plans for welfare and not for evil, to give you a future and a hope, **Jeremiah 29:11**.

Many times God will give us a vision of what needs to be done, but may not give us each and every step that needs to be taken, and even there, God is faithful. Commit your work to the Lord, and your plans will be established **Proverbs 16:3**.

You might be asking what does this have to do with paid in full, void, null. The answer is we have an adversary that also likes to try and direct our steps and mess up what God is trying to do in our lives and when we do mess up, this adversary accuses us of being a mess up. Be sober-minded; be watchful. Your adversary, the devil prowls around like a roaring lion, seeking someone to devour **Peter 5:8**. And often times we think we are being led in the right direction, but it is really not what God wants for our lives and we are being deceived. And no wonder, for even Satan disguises himself as an angel of light, **2 Corinthians 11:14**.

Here's where we can rejoice, God always has us covered and He will never tear us down, but lift us up. The enemy not only accuses us before the Father, but he reminds us of how badly we mess up and probably on a regular basis. And I heard a loud voice in heaven, saying, "Now the salvation, the power and the kingdom of our God and the authority of his Christ have come, for the accuser of our brothers has been thrown down, who accuses them day and night before our God, **Revelation 12:10**.

What does it mean to be an accuser? It means someone who is a faultfinder and criticizer, so the enemy is finding fault with our actions and is criticizing what we do, how we do it before the Lord God Almighty and when that doesn't work, he gets us turning on ourselves.

So the enemy comes with our guilty ticket which has to be paid according to the law, but what we get rather than a sentence for the offense, we get a notice telling us while each one of us had a crushing sin debt, Jesus paid it in full for us through his death on the cross. We are told the Bible says Jesus "himself bore our sins in his body on the tree….the righteous for the unrighteous, that he might bring us to God." (**1 Peter 2:24, 3:18**). That means Jesus paid for all of my sins—past, present and future. Any ticket I get for a sin committed has been paid in full and when the enemy goes before the Father accusing, faultfinding and criticizing us of a wrong doing and handing God a ticket on our behalf, it gets stamped, null and void because the price for the offense has been paid in full. That's "has been" past tense, not will be or might be or could be. It has been done.

And you know, if the enemy can't get God to condemn us, he tries to get us to condemn ourselves, and often times, we are harder on ourselves than God would ever be on us. It's times like this when we are beating ourselves up that we need to remind ourselves that we have a clean record, the penalty for the sin has been paid for by another and when we do sin it's not the norm, but the exception to the rule. We are told in **Ephesians 2:2** in which you once walked, following the course of this world, following the prince of the power of the air, the spirit that is now at work in the sons of disobedience. The key is once walked, meaning it used to be the norm, but now, I am a son of the Living God and not a son of disobedience, so my sins are exceptions to the rule, not a way of life and when I do mess up, thank God I can lean on **1 John 1:9;** if we confess our sins, he is faithful and just to forgive us our sins and to cleanse us

176

from all unrighteousness. **Psalm 32:5;** I acknowledged my sin to you, and I did not cover my iniquity; I said, "I will confess my transgressions to the Lord," and you forgave the iniquity of my sin and finally, **1 John 2:1;** My little children, I am writing these things to you so that you may not sin. But if anyone does sin, we have an advocate with the Father, Jesus Christ the righteous. My friend, Jesus Christ the righteous, is the one who stamped our ticket, the reminder of the transgression, the go to jail and do not pass go card with the words, this offense has been paid in full, this ticket is no longer valid, it is void and null, although important and deserving of a guilty sentence, this person can go free and their record is clean and clear of the offense, they no longer have to carry the yolk of heaviness, they are free to leave, and that, my friend, is the best news we could ever hear.

Prayer: Father, I've heard the story of how you paid in full my debt of sin, but help me to get it from my head deep down in to my heart, internalize it and live it out.

1. Do you fully understand what Christ did for you on the cross and how your debt was wiped clean?
2. Has anyone ever paid a bill for you or have you ever paid off another person's bill, and if so, how did it make you feel?

Week 38
Amazing, Absolutely Amazing

Our second night back in the land, I was lying in bed looking at the ceiling just thinking about the past events of so many years. Ever have one of those moments where you just stare at the ceiling as you reminisce over what God has done and is doing in your life, your family and your circumstances? Well, that's what I was doing. I turned to Norma, who was trying to sleep and I said 'it's amazing, absolutely amazing what God has been doing with us.' Here we are sleeping in Israel, three days ago, we were sleeping in Germany, three months ago, we were sleeping in Georgia, four months ago we were sleeping in Virginia and it just went on and on and on. I can remember sleeping in France, Italy and Mexico

I can also remember when we had a home and a car and what was considered a normal life and all that came to a close when we got that heavenly call. What amazed me was not the amount of traveling that we do or how we have given up everything that we owned, but the faithfulness of God in the midst of our lives and how He is always there faithfully to help us. I realized and am still realizing that God is in the supply business. It is his desire to supply our needs, wants and desires. Why not, He supplied the first man and woman a garden where all their needs were met. He even tells us in **Philippians 4:19** and this same God who takes care of me will supply all your needs from his glorious riches, which have been given to us in Christ Jesus.

You know, I have discovered that I have needs that I'm not even aware of, needs which are not even on my mind or in my thought process and yet my God supplies, listen to this, all my needs, even the ones that I don't know about. Now, that is a considerate and thoughtful God. I mean it's as if God said "here, you're going to need this in a few days, so I'm supplying it for you now." What am I going to say? Really? How do you know? He could say as He did in **Matthew 6:32,** For the pagans run after all these things, and your heavenly Father knows that you need them, or in **Isaiah 46:10,** He tells us: From the beginning I revealed the end. From long ago I told you things that had not yet happened, saying, "My plan will stand, and I'll do everything I intended to do." In other words, He knows ours needs before there is a need and what God supplies are never wrong. Maybe the way we use them is wrong, but He is never wrong with what we need and when we need it.

I have an old saying that tells me, 'when we get involved in God's business, He will get involved in our businesses. So here I am lying in bed absolutely amazed how God has supplied our needs through the many years and used precious saints to continue His work. You know, I use the word saints, but truth be told, it's a family of believers who have been indelibly inscribed on our hearts. Friends come and go, but family members are with you for the rest of your life and God has given us a family that live all over the world. I could talk about the family of God in length, but that would be another message.

So God is the supplier of all good things in our lives and not only good things but He also supplies it in abundance as He tells us in **Ephesians 3:20**, Glory belongs to God, whose power is at work in us. By this power, he can do exceeding, abundantly, infinitely above all that we can ask or imagine. I've learned that our God is so amazing. He doesn't do things exceedingly which I would be happy with nor does He do things abundantly which I would be thrilled about, but He does all things exceedingly abundantly. That has to be more than enough for any situation or need that confronts us today.

Think about that and then think on **2 Corinthians 9:8,** And God is able to bless you abundantly, so that in all things at all times, having all that you need, you will abound in every good work. My friends, God is for us, not against us. He wants us to win at every stage of our life and not just win, but with all the blessing of heaven. If that were not true, why would He who is not a man that He should lie tell us in **Ephesians 1:3,** Praise the God and Father of our Lord Jesus Christ! Through Christ, God has blessed us with every spiritual blessing that heaven has to offer.

So as I lay in bed amazed with God because He has blessed us abundantly with all that we need, at all times and in all things because we are doing His good work. When God signs the contract that we are employed in His service, He really treats His employees well, never goes back on His word, never fires us, has a great medical plan, amazing benefits that keep on giving 24/7 hotline to His presence and a retirement plan in an amazing retirement location with not just a vacation home but a mansion, can you imagine that? God is more than enough.

Prayer: Gracious Father, you have done so many things in my life and have delivered me from so many situations that I'm aware of and also not aware of. Please give me a heart of thanksgiving for all that you do for me and let me be a vessel of praise.

1. Do you sometimes take for granted what God has done for you throughout your life?
2. Do you believe that God has delivered you from situations that may have been very harmful to you and yet He remained totally and completed unidentified?
3. Is your life like the book of Esther, where the name of God is never mentioned? Why did you answer the way you did?

Week 39
All My Fountains Are in You

Not too long ago, I was sitting in our dear friend's backyard and my mind wandered back to when Norma and I were attending the Chesapeake Vineyard. What a great memory that was. Anyway, I was remembering all the good friends we had and the times we experienced there. One of my very good friends was a brother named, John, who has gone on to be with the Lord. John loved to praise the Lord and one of his and my favorite songs was 'No Other' by David Ruis. During the song, there was a line that repeated itself and was both John's and my favorite line, which said; all, all my fountains are in You. Actually, this is from scripture, in **Psalm 87:7,** we are told, as they make music, they will sing, "All my fountains are in you."

As I thought about this song, many things flooded my mind. For one, I really appreciated and missed my brother very much but was very happy to know that one day we will be re-united. Not only re-united with John, but with all my dear friends and family members that have graduated and now see Him face-to-face.

There's another song out there that says; I can only imagine. The good news is those who have gone on to be with the Lord don't have to imagine, they see Him face-to-face, it's the rest of us that can only imagine.

Anyway, I was thinking about those words that John use to sing, All my fountains are in You and it dawned on me, all my fountains really are in Him. You know another word for a fountain is spring, source or origin.

As I thought about it, it was very true that all my sources and origins are in God. The only thing I can do without Him is fail.

Interesting, in scripture a well of water, or a fountain, is often linked as being the Word of God, and also doctrine from the Word of God, and therefore truth itself. So whenever we see a well or fountain in scripture that doesn't have any water, we are looking at something that is dried up and not able to sustain one.

Example, in **Jeremiah 2:13,** we are told "For my people have done two evil things: They have abandoned me--the fountain of living water. And they have dug for themselves cracked cisterns that can hold no water. By the way, a cistern is nothing more than a large water container. The problem is, before they would look to God for their water and now they were looking to their own achievements or abilities to gather water.

But it wasn't only water that gave life, but the doctrines of God which was truth as well. Here's the problem, when you have a doctrine that has no truth, what you have is a pit, or a well with no water and a waterless pit denotes doctrines that are not true; and broken pits, which are fabricated doctrines, and therefore, false.

In **Jeremiah 14:3**, we are told; "Their nobles have sent their servants for water; they have come to the cisterns or

183

pits and found no water. They have returned with their vessels empty; they have been put to shame and humiliated, and they cover their heads.

In **Proverbs 14:27,** we are encouraged with the fear of the LORD is a fountain of life, turning a person from the snares of death. Again in **Psalm 36:9** for with You is the fountain of life; In Your light we see light.

You see my friends, God is the fountain of life, and as **John 7:38** tells us; whoever believes in me, as the Scripture has said, 'Out of his inner being will flow rivers of living water.'

As I thought about this, I told myself; God is the fountain of life; in Him is everything I will ever have a need for. What else is there that I will ever need if God is my all sufficiency?

As I am fond of saying, everything I have God gave me, but God hasn't given me everything that He has. Truly, I can proclaim and declare with **Psalm 87:7,** all my fountains are in you and this isn't just a memory verse, but a declaration of life, and because of that I can say all my sources or origins or beginnings are in God and why would I even consider trying to have something which is apart from my creator.

Separation or doing anything apart from God doesn't bring joy, but just the opposite. Look at reward for allowing God to be your fountain of life, **Revelation 7:16, 17;** they will hunger no longer, nor thirst anymore; nor will the sun beat down on them, nor any heat; for the Lamb in the center of the throne will be their shepherd, and will guide them to springs of the water of life; and God will wipe every tear from their eyes.

With God, there is no need for any other. As the song that we started out with continues, another line says; there is no other friend like you, oh Lord, there is no other love like You, oh Lord and the line ends with it must be You.

To which I can only add my amen, God, it must be You because all I have is You, all my hope is in You, all I wish to accomplish is in You, God and God alone is my Fountain of Life and with You I will never return with empty vessels; and never be put to shame and humiliated, and I will never have to cover my head.

Prayer: Father, help me to come to the place where I realize that the only thing I can do successfully without you is fail. Everything I have and all that I am is because of who you are and teach me to be thankful for how intimately involved you are in my life.

1. Do you sometimes go through the day completely unaware that God is going before you and behind you? Why is that?
2. Jesus said I will never leave you nor forsake you, but be with you always. In light of that promise, do you sometimes take Jesus places that he would rather not have gone or said things he would rather not have heard?

3. Do you think that you sometimes take Jesus, the King of kings and Lord of lord for granted and totally ignore Him? Justify your response.

Week 40
Free Indeed

The Lord was speaking to me concerning today's teaching and He was doing it in so many ways that it was impossible to miss what God was trying to say. The other day I was watching a movie and there was a particular scene where a full grown gorilla that was born in captivity and raised its entire life in a cage was finally given its freedom. The gorilla's handlers unlocked the cage and opened the cage door and stood back to see what would happen. The gorilla came up to the door and just stood there gazing out from the opened gate. After about five minutes, he turned around and went back inside the safety of the cage without ever stepping outside of the cage.

It reminded me so much of the verse found in **Luke 24:2,** and they found the stone rolled away from the tomb. I've come to the conclusion that rolling the stone away is the easy part, getting the people to step out of the darkness in to the light or out of death in to life is the hard part. You see, my friend, freedom is not a physical issue; it's a mental and spiritual issue. An open cage door or a stone rolled away doesn't make you free any more than being locked up defines you as being captive.

While teaching at a prison in Florida, I asked some of the Christ believing prisoners about their incarceration and to my surprise the answer was that in Jesus they are experiencing a greater freedom in prison than they have ever experienced outside of prison. The reason for their statement is really simple, so much so that it was recorded in an old hymn that asks the question:

 Would you be free from your burden of sin? Again it asks, would you be free from your passion and pride? And the answer for their deliverance is:

There's power in the blood, power in the blood;
There's wonderful power in the blood.
There is power, power, wonder-working power,
In the blood of the Lamb.

And because of that, each prisoner was able to come for a cleansing to Calvary's tide, why, because there's wonderful power in the blood.

These prisoners were free from their burden of sin, their passion and pride. These young men were free for one reason and only one reason, and the reason can be found in **John 8:36,** so if the Son sets you free, you are truly free.

So back to the gorilla in the cage, was he free? No, not at all, he was a prisoner locked up in an open cage because his mind told his body or how ever gorillas think, that he was still locked up in a cage.

Many believers have been told that Jesus came to set them free, and for too many, it's just a wonderful memory verse, but they have not truly experienced the freedom of being free from whatever is holding them in bondage. Many are in a mental cage that has its doors open, but because of things that have happened in their past or because of unforgiveness or curses spoken against them in their childhood, they are still in bondage and the idea of being free because of the wonder-working power of the blood of the Lamb is always just beyond their reach. The stone has been rolled aside and Jesus has given the invitation to step out of the darkness into His glorious light and fear has kept you from accepting that invitation.

My friend, if this is describing you in any way, I break that curse and rebuke what the enemy has been doing in your life. I declare and proclaim freedom in the name of Jesus. I state that that freedom will rise up in you like a mighty fountain that cannot be contained.

One other thing my friends, you cannot walk in God given freedom without God given peace. We are told in **John 14:27,** peace I leave with you; my peace I give you. I do not give to you as the world gives. Do not let your hearts be troubled and do not be afraid. True peace is not the absence of conflict, but to be whole and complete. If you are whole and complete in Jesus, you can be in the midst of anything and have the peace which exceeds all understanding. How can I do that you might be thinking? Because it's not the world's peace, but the peace of God that was given you. You see, my friend; God is the Master that we can serve in perfect freedom and perfect peace.

We are commanded to live in peace, but because of the winds and waves of life, many of us are living in pieces. We are children of the light, His glorious light and a benefit of that light is freedom. Sure things may come against us and try to rob of us that God given freedom, but we are told in **Galatians 5:1,** Christ has freed us so that we may enjoy the benefits of freedom. Therefore, be firm [in this freedom], and don't become slaves again. You might be asking yourself; how do I not become a slave again to that thing that has been stealing my freedom and peace. The answer to that can be found in **John 8:32,** and you will know the truth, and the truth will set you free.

Let me say this, truth is not a thing, truth is a person and that person has a name and that name is Jesus and He confirms this in **John 14:6,** when He tells us; Jesus answered, "I am the way and the truth and the life.

If you desire to live a life of real freedom and peace, there is a way and it's called Jesus, there is a truth and it's Jesus and there is a life, it's still this same Jesus. Jesus will show you the way and reveal the truth and give you an abundant life.

Prayer: Lord, you have told me in your word that you have set me free. Help me to walk in the freedom that as a child of the living God rightfully belongs to me and to realize that freedom is not because of what I do, but because of what you did.

1. The Lord said He has set you free, are you really walking in that freedom?
2. What are some of the things that keep you bound and not experiencing true freedom?
3. In light of question 2, what would be the steps to walk in Christ-centered, God fearing freedom?

Week 41
Double Filling

If you are a believer in Jesus Christ, then you are blessed beyond words. Why you might be asking yourself? Because God is moving and bringing major revivals all around the world and touching the lives of the spiritually hungry. God does this either individually as He is doing with many Muslims in the Middle East or God is doing it corporately as He has done with Catch the Fire in Canada or the Brownsville revival or what God is doing in Bethel Temple in California.

Let's face it, God can move anyway; He wants and usually does and never needs our permission, just our obedience.

Have you ever thought to yourself; I sure wish God would move here in my church or my city with signs and wonders the way He does overseas? Or wondered why week after week, the services in my home church are the same ole, same ole. I guess the answer to those questions is does God have a platform to move the way He wants to move without the programs and schedules that typically binds his hands.

Do we try to put God in a box, wrap it up with pretty bows and spiritualize it by calling it revival? Truly **Isaiah 55:8,** is very true when God tells us; "My thoughts are nothing like your thoughts," says the LORD. "And my ways are far beyond anything you could imagine."

Why is it we as a people are willing to go to other places to receive whatever the other places have to offer? It's common sense to think we will travel to Florida to be entertained by Disney or travel out west to be thrilled by the view of the great Red Wood trees or travel to distant parts of the world to see the beautiful sights of new and exciting nations, but often when it comes to the things of God we say, Lord, pass this way or manifest yourself here in our building?

This brings me to an interesting point in **Luke 5:4-7**. When he had finished speaking, he said to Simon, "Put out into deep water, and let down the nets for a catch." Simon answered, "Master, we've worked hard all night and haven't caught anything. But because you say so, I will let down the nets." When they had done so, they caught such a large number of fish that their nets began to break. So they signaled their partners in the other boat to come and help them, and they came and filled both boats so full that they began to sink.

The entire passage is amazing but what really blessed me was the part that says; so they signaled their partners in the other boat to come and help them, and they came and filled both boats so full that they began to sink.

It's easy to see that we have a miracle here and it's obvious that God's direct intervention is taking place. The other boat could have spiritualized the entire scene and said, God, why don't you pass by here and fill us with what you're doing, why is it that miracles always happen somewhere else? They could have thought or even said that, but they went to where the Lord was doing something. Were they filled? Of course, almost to the point to where they began to sink.

Sometimes, my friend, when we hear that God is moving powerfully in another place, state or church, we need to stop asking Him that when He's done, would He mind stopping by our church and fill us, but rather make for the door and go to where God is moving and be touched and filled by what He's doing someplace else.

Did the second boat leave the fishes in the boat? Of course not, they brought the entire catch back to land and did with them what they always do with them. When you are touched by God, do you leave the miracle in that other place? Of course not, you bring it back to where you came from with shouts of testimony and let's do here what we did there.

God fills you for a purpose and it's not to store up and keep it to yourself, but pass to it on. **Hebrews 13:16** tells us; and don't forget to do good and to share with those in need. These are the sacrifices that please God. I'm sure we are all in need of what God is doing around the world for none of us have arrived when it comes to being filled with the fullness of what God is doing. Isn't this the reason why when people go on mission trips abroad and are used to laying hands on the sick and seeing healings and miracles take place with their own hands that they come back home all pumped up, excited and ready to do the same thing at home like they did overseas? Isn't this the reason why when people come back from say Catch the Fire in Toronto that they become excited to pass on with their congregation or home group what they saw God doing in Canada? Why? Because their spiritual boats were filled to almost sinking and they got to share it with others.

My friend, no one is saying leave your congregation, but I am saying that if God is moving powerfully somewhere else and you feel the need to go for a filling, then I say go, get filled and bring it back to where there's a need in your own group. Remember, we are all just vessels to be used by the Holy Spirit and we don't take credit for what God is doing through us any more than the hose takes credit for putting out the fire.

Prayer: Lord, you are able and willing to move anywhere you want to bring about revival in the hearts of those who need your presence. Help me to be part of your movement and to be part of the solution and not the problems in people's lives.

1. Do you ever think to yourself; God you move in Africa and in China, how come you don't move like that here in America? What can you do to be used in a Godly movement?

Week 42
No One Cares

I remember on numerous occasions when I was just a kid growing up in New York City that I would rush home and tell my two older brothers about what happened to me during the day or what I saw on my adventures around the neighborhood or why I was sent to the principal's office in school and it was usually followed by that old familiar statement: "shut-up, no one cares".

Maybe I would meet with my little Our Gang Comedy group of friends and tell them about my adventures since we were all about the same age, 11 years old. Our little group also had a familiar saying of which we were all guilty, really? Who cares? I once tried that in school with the teacher when she asked me a math question and I said really? Who cares? And that was enough to send me back to the principal's office, of course my friends thought I was the bravest person in the world. How wrong they were.

Have you ever had a heavy issue and you were pouring out your heart to someone only to feel like they could care less about what you were going through? I mean the feedback you got and the lack of sensitivity to your issue seems to shout out: no one cares or really? Who cares?

The mind can play funny games with you, and many times, you even ask yourself the question: does anyone really care about what I'm going through? You might even say to yourself: I wish they could be in my shoes just to see how hard or painful this situation is and then they would be more sensitive to my concerns or maybe they would just listen to my heart and what I'm trying to say without even responding.

You know, we don't always have to have a response or a comeback to a person's conversation. I remember visiting a person in the hospital who had cancer. They just wanted to talk, they didn't want a response or suggestion or great idea. What they wanted was someone to be with them, company and a listening ear not a speaking mouth. In other words, they wanted to be with someone that they thought cared about what they had to say or what they were going through.

A good question for you and for me is: Is there anyone that really, really cares about what we go through or cares about us in general and not superficial caring, but from the deepest part of the heart caring? And the answer comes back with a resounding yes.

You see the real question that we dare not ask when we are in the darkest place of our life and seemingly things can't get any worse is: Does God really care. We know that God is love, but when we are in the deepest darkness and our prayers seem to be bouncing off a brass ceiling with no response, we often think or say out loud, God do you care or are you even there?

In my 71 years of life, I have learned that good things happen to bad people and bad things happen to good people. I've learned that it rains on the just the same way it rains on the unjust. But I've also learned that as a child of the living God when I cry out to my heavenly Father, He hears my prayers and when I give God all the choices of my life, He will always make the best decision for my life.

As I was reading in **Psalm 107: 27-31,** it said: They reeled and staggered like a drunken man, and were at their wits' end. Then they cried to the LORD in their trouble, And He brought them out of their distresses. He caused the storm to be still, So that the waves of the sea were hushed, then they were glad because they were quiet, So He guided them to their desired haven. Let them give thanks to the LORD for His loving kindness, And for His wonders to the sons of men!

Why would the Lord God Almighty cause the waves of the sea to be stilled? Because He cares about the conditions of men both in ancient times and today. I'm sure someone might be asking themselves can I expect God to deliver me today in 2016 just like He did to those men in Old Testament times. We find the answer in **Romans 2:11**: "For there is no partiality with God" and God is the same yesterday, today and forever, He does not change.

You've heard the expression: the proof is in the pudding. In other words, the proof that God cares for us for us is evidenced by the gift of His son to die for our sins.

Paul wrote in **Romans 8:31-32**, "What then shall we say to these things? If God be for us, who can be against us? He who did not spare His own Son, but delivered Him up for us all, how shall He not with Him also freely give us all things?"

Peter confirms our assurance that our Lord cares when he wrote in **I Peter 5:7**, "Casting all your care upon Him; for He cares for you."

Let me say this, you are not just a face in the crowd. It's very natural to ask, "Why me?" when pain and confusion and trouble come into your life. And the reality is it often seems so unfair. I'm sure we might think to ourselves, why do some people's lives seem so pain-free, while terrible things happen to others? Why is it in the same accident, some will walk away unhurt, while others lose their lives. Why? Why does God seemingly work a miracle for some—but not for others? Doesn't He care?

I'm sorry to say, but a totally satisfying answer to such questions does not exist. We must remember, however, that in the end, the power of miracles—and the reasons for them—remain in God's hands, and God's alone. You might even say: I don't understand. This is why we are told in **Ecclesiastes 5:2** "God is in heaven and you are on earth, so let your words be few." God allows things to happen to us to strengthen our faith, not to question it.

Does God really care for us? He cares about you and me so much so that we are told in **John 3:16,** for this is the way God loved the world: He gave his one and only Son, so that everyone who believes in him will not perish but have eternal life. This is confirmed in **1 John 4:9,** God showed how much he loved us by sending his one and only Son into the world so that we might have eternal life through him. We are also told in **Romans 5:5,** and hope does not disappoint us, because God has poured out His love into our hearts through the Holy Spirit, whom He has given us.

How many times does God have to say something in order for it to be true? Only once and yet God has repeated Himself over and over and over to show you that His love and care for you have no boundaries. If you have a doubt about God's love based on what you are going through, my friend, you need to bring closure to that. The enemy can bring about alienation which means isolation and separation from God because of your doubts which are not from God, but based on your experiences and your battle in the mind.

A great promise to keep in mind can be found in **I Peter 5:6-7**. Therefore humble yourselves under the mighty hand of God, that He may exalt you at the proper time, casting all your worries, concerns, anxiety and fears on Him, because He cares for you.

Prayer: Father, help me to really understand that when friends or family turn their back on me, You will never turn your back or leave me or abandon me, that is your promise to me.

1. Do you sometimes cast your cares or problems on the Lord only to take them back when things don't go the way you thought they would go? Why?
2. Have you ever tried to do something your own way only to realize that God's way would have been faster and more efficient?

Week 43
Life is Still Good, Regardless

The other day, I was thinking about one thing when the Lord reminded me of an expression I had used many years ago and I heard in my mind; there are many things worse than dying.

As I was remembering this expression, I was also reminded of the situation that brought about the expression. I was speaking to a friend who was complaining about everything that was wrong with the world, his family, his job, his life his income and everything else that he could think of. By the way, this friend was a believer. It's just that at this point in his life, he was believing a lot of things that were taking away his joy and peace.

I'm sure we have all been at that place one time or another and I'm also pretty sure that we are really glad to have left that place where it would seem a dark cloud is always following us wherever we go.

That place is a really difficult place because, although, we know what the Word of God says and we know that **Numbers 23:19** is true, which tells us; God is not like people. He tells no lies. He is not like humans. He doesn't change his mind. When he says something, he does it. When he makes a promise, he keeps it, we know this is absolutely true, but it would seem that the problems are bigger than the promises. Why is this place a really difficult place? Because we have to hold on to the promises of God when everything around us seems to be

contradicting what God has been telling us. Because at this
season in your life, it would seem that life really stinks and
everything that could go wrong is going wrong, and out of
desperation, we try to figure out a way to get out of this
season and realize that our efforts are now becoming part of
the problem and not the solution.

To buttress that, we look at **Psalms 63:3,** Because Your
loving-kindness is better than life, My lips shall praise You
and we tell ourselves; right now Lord, life stinks, I don't
see your loving-kindness and the last thing on my mind, not
my heart is to praise You.

So, my friend, the question becomes; what do we do?
There are many cliché expressions that, although, difficult
to put in to action, are really very true. When given a
lemon make lemonade or when at the end of your rope
make a knot and hang on. Kind of reminds me of a story
about a young man who inadvertently fell off a cliff and
was able to grab a hold of a limb on the way down the side
of the mountain. Holding on to this limb with his arms
stretched out on top of him, unable to look down or to the
side, he cried out to the Lord for help. Help Lord, Help, he
cried until he heard a voice say; let go. Again, he cried out,
help Lord and again he heard; let go. This time the young
man cried out, is there anyone else up there? Again he
heard let go. This time the young man said, Lord, I guess
it's time to come home to you, so please take care of my
family and friends, and with that, he lets go of the limb,
only to find that he was two feet from the ground.

Some of us feel like we are holding on to the limb, and every time we cry out to the Lord to help us and deliver us, what we hear is let go. My friend, do you realize that to obey God is to give the only visible evidence that you really believe God? Let me say that one more time in a different way, your obedience to God is the only evidence you have that you really and truly believe God.

In **Isaiah 1:18,** the first part of the verse tells us; "Come now, let us reason together, says the LORD" another version says; "Come, let us discuss this," says the LORD" a third version and one I like very much says; Come, let's consider your options," says the LORD. The thing that really jumps off the page to me is the little word "us" which means to refer to the speaker and another person, or one person and another person with the original person.

So what this means is with all the lousy situations going on in life, when we call out to the Lord, He replies with, why don't the two of us, that's you and Me take a look at all your options and let's talk about them. That, my friend, is an invitation from God to share with what's going on in our lives. It's like the scepter of the King of Kings to enter the throne room, sit down and just talk.

So we say; God I don't like what's going on and He tells us in **Matthew 11:28,** come to me, all you that labor and are heavy laden, and I will give you rest. We say God, it's taking away my peace and joy and He tells us in **1 Peter 5:7,** cast all your anxiety on Me because I care for you. We say, God I feel like I'm in this dark tunnel of life all alone and He tells us; **Psalm 68:19,** Praise be to the Lord, to God our Savior, who daily bears our burdens. Who knows, there may be some of you that say something like in **Psalm 13:2,** how long must I make decisions alone with sorrow in my heart day after day? How long will my enemy triumph over me? And God reassures us with: **Deuteronomy 31:8,** do not be afraid or discouraged, for the LORD will personally go ahead of you. He will be with you; he will neither fail you nor abandon you." Another version says it even cleared; The LORD is the one who is going ahead of you. He will be with you. He won't abandon you or leave you. So don't be afraid or terrified."

So my friends, what is the thought position of a believer going through hard times:

You are not there by mistake. **Psalm 37:23,** a person's steps are directed by the LORD, and the LORD delights in his way. This day is not a mistake. **Psalm 118:24,** this is the day the LORD has made; let us rejoice and be glad in it. You are not in this alone. **Deuteronomy 31:8,** the LORD himself goes before you and will be with you; he will never leave you nor forsake you. Do not be afraid; do not be discouraged. This situation will turn out okay. **Romans 8:28,** "And we know that God causes all things to work together for good to those who love God, to those who are called according to His purpose." God's plans for your life are much better than your plans for your life. **Jeremiah 29:11,** "I know the plans that I have for you, declares the LORD. They are plans for peace and not disaster; plans to give you a future filled with hope."

My friends, like every other tunnel that you have been through in life, God is still there with you, He's still faithful to get you through this season and you are still the head, not the tail, still on top, not the bottom, still more than a conqueror not a loser, still a winner not a loser and still in the palm of a loving heavenly Father.

Knowing all that, we are also able to declare as it says in **Psalms 63:3**: Because Your loving-kindness is better than life, My lips shall praise You.

Prayer: Father, I've looked at my life before I knew you and also when I became one of your children and I see that your loving kindness is truly a life filled with the joy of the Lord. Help me to always be mindful of the benefits of walking with you as your child.

1. Have you ever felt that trying to walk a Godly walk is just too much hard work and you can't do it anyway? What are your options to walking with God?
2. Do you really think that without God in your life, you could be successful in all you do?
3. Why is it so hard to give God control of your life? How would you start to give up control?

Week 44
Whose Name is Above all Names?

Have you ever noticed when we get in to a situation that we don't want to be in, we try and do everything in our power to either make it go away or try to get control over it so we can be on the top of it and not under its influence? Have you also noticed that often times while trying to bring the whole mess under control, we end up becoming part of the problem and not the solution?

Sometimes, although meaning well, we end up pouring gasoline on the fire and not water, meaning we cause a mountain to spring up when it was originally just a little bump in the road, and all because we wanted to be over the circumstances and not under the circumstances.

If I had to take an educated guess, I would say that its human nature to try and always be in control over one's circumstances in life, always to be on the top and not the bottom, always to be the head and not the tail.

Granted, the Word of God tells us in **Deuteronomy 28:13,** the LORD will make you the head, not the tail. If you pay attention to the commands of the LORD your God that I give you this day and carefully follow them, you will always be at the top, never at the bottom. We are also reminded in **Proverbs 3:5 & 6,** Trust in the LORD with all your heart and do not lean on your own understanding. In all your ways, acknowledge Him, and He will make your paths straight.

We learn from scripture that we can be winners and not losers, we can be the head and not the tail, and we can always be at the top and not at the bottom, but not in our own strength, not in our own wisdom and craftiness and cunning devices. Our place of victory is not out of a position of strength, but out of a position of self-realization that without Christ, we are weak. As a matter of fact, the only thing we can do without Jesus is fail.

We are encouraged to trust in the LORD with all our heart and do not lean on our own understanding and we are told that for a very important reason. We are not in control of the destiny of our lives. Our names are not the names that are above all names. It's for this reason that it is revealed in **Ephesians 1:21, 22,** "That God raised Jesus from the dead and seated Him at His right hand in the heavenly places, far above all rule, authority, power and dominion, and every name that is named, not only in this age, but also in the one to come. And He put all things in subjection under His feet, and gave Him as head over all things to the church." Just so we understand what was just said, it's repeated in **Philippians 2:9,** therefore, God exalted him meaning Jesus to the highest place and gave him, Jesus, the name that is above every name.

As mentioned, we are often part of the problem and not the solution because although we mean well, we don't have the full picture of what's going on in our lives. We have limited understanding, wisdom and ability to see the ending from the beginning. Yet, it is stated in **Job 12:13** with him is wisdom and strength, he has counsel and understanding.

And again in **Daniel 2:20,** "Praise be to the name of God for ever and ever; wisdom and power are his."

When they speak of God having strength, power and wisdom, what are they actually saying? When it says strength, it means that God has complete force, might, security, majesty, boldness and praise (believe me, there is power in praise). When it tells us wisdom, it also means God has complete sound knowledge, success, efficient wisdom, abiding success, intellectual understanding and the ability to help in all matters.

We should be able to rest in God's great ability, but we can also ask why and how is God able to do all this through Jesus? Simple, because God raised Jesus from the dead and seated Him at His right hand in the heavenly places, far above all rules, authority, power and dominion, and every name that is named, not only in this age, but also in the one to come. And He put all things in subjection under His feet, and gave Him as head over all things to the church.

What does that mean? It means there's no sense in doing double work. If there are any situations in our lives that are out of our control, there is already One who has it under control. If there are circumstances that we have no idea what the next step is, there is One who knows exactly what the next step is. If your life is falling apart and every effort you did to fix it has failed, there is One who knows more of your future than you know of your past and He is more than able and more than willing to put all the pieces together to make a new you, a new family and a new creation. If you give Him all the choices in your life, He will make the best

207

decision for you, your life and your family. Oh, and one more thing, it's a trinity not a forth some and He doesn't need your help unless He asks you to get involved.

Prayer: Lord, it's so easy to get over-whelmed with all the titles and names and positions that people have tagged themselves with. Help me to keep my eyes on the only one that has the Name above all Names and if I keep my eyes on the invisible, I will be able to do the impossible.

1. Do you sometimes think that you would like to have a big title? Why?
2. We are told that King David stripped off all his priestly robes, meaning his titles before the Lord. Why do you think he did that?
3. Do you really believe that God is impressed with all your titles? Justify your answer.

Week 45
Friends

The other day I was thinking back on how many really good and close friends I have. I realized a few things and one of them was distance and time, do not affect the quality of a true friend.

Granted, you enjoy being with a good friend, but you don't always have to be together or live nearby to be or have a true friend.

I have a few true friends that, although, we stay in contact, we haven't seen each other for many years and when we do have the opportunity to visit one another, it was as if the conversation picked up where it ended many years ago and our being together seemed so very right.

Another point is if there was a crisis with either one of us, we knew beyond a shadow of a doubt that the other person would be there as a moral, physical and mental support to see each other through the crisis. As a matter of fact, a true friend doesn't even have to say much when you are with them. You're very happy just with their presence, not so much their conversation although what they have to say is important to you not only because of what they said, but because of who is speaking.

One last thing about a true friend; they will stick closer to you than a family member and they will either speak the truth to you in love even if it's painful when they see a flaw in your behavior or they will receive correction if you need to speak in to their life.

When I say a true friend, I don't mean an acquaintance or even a friend or good friend, and definitely not a fair weather friend which brings me to the reason for this message.

I was reading in Acts the story where we are told that Paul and Barnabas were in Lystra and there sat a man who was lame. He had been that way from birth and had never walked. He listened to Paul as he was speaking. (Let me interrupt for just a second and say this man had never walked and he was hearing Paul speak about the Lord. If you want to see more miracles in your life or your ministry, try speaking more about Jesus and what you say just might be the seed of faith in a person to receive the healing they are waiting for). Paul looked directly at him, saw that he had faith to be healed and called out, and stand up on your feet! At that, the man jumped up and began to walk. (One other observation, It didn't say the man had to join a church or go to a seminar or read the first four books of the gospel or even have oil poured on him, or hands laid upon him, although these are not wrong but it's not a formula, don't put how God moves in a box). When the crowd saw what Paul had done, they shouted in the Lycaonian language, "The gods have come down to us in human form!" Barnabas they called Zeus, and Paul they called Hermes because he was the chief speaker. The priest of Zeus, whose temple was just outside the city, brought bulls and wreaths to the city gates because he and the crowd wanted to offer sacrifices to them (**Acts 14: 8-13**).

That sounds to me like Paul and Barnabas were big shots and really important to the people of the city. Talk about a ticker tape parade down Main Street Lystra and getting the keys to the city.

Kind of reminds me of another story found in **Matthew 21**. We're told that the disciples went and did as Jesus had instructed them. They brought the donkey and the colt and placed their cloaks on them for Jesus to sit on. A very large crowd spread their cloaks on the road, while others cut branches from the trees and spread them on the road. The crowds that went ahead of him and those that followed shouted, "Hosanna to the Son of David!" "Blessed is he who comes in the name of the Lord!" "Hosanna in the highest heaven!" When Jesus entered Jerusalem, the whole city was stirred and asked, "Who is this?" The crowds answered, "This is Jesus, the prophet from Nazareth in Galilee." **Matthew 21:6-11**.

Talk about being thought of as a big shot and having the keys to the city. Granted, it was never Jesus's intention, but regardless, He was the reason for the ticker tape parade down Main Street Jerusalem.

Just because the population masses seems to recognize how special and important you are and yells out Hosanna in your name or offers to sacrifice animals to how special you are and bring wreaths in your honor doesn't make them friends. Being familiar with the ending of **Matthew 21 and Acts 14**, we know the cry of the mob is very fickle and changes on a heartbeat from Hosanna one day to crucify

Him the next day or here we have bulls and wreaths in your honor one hour and stone him until He's dead the next hour.

I'm going to take a wild guess here and say these were not crowds of friends. Maybe for a moment they acted as fair weather friends or by definition, a friend who is only a friend when circumstances are pleasant or profitable. At the first sign of trouble, these unpredictable, disloyal friends will drop their relationship with you.

And please, don't get me wrong, I'm not saying there weren't true friends in the crowd that day, but it would seem the majority had the power to sway the authorities to their way of thinking and all because a minority turned the tide for the majority. Isn't it amazing how gossip can turn the course of history by planting seeds of discourse and how quickly that can happen?

It's great to have friends and to be a friend, but it's more important to have a good and true friend. As a matter of fact, friends are so important that the bible is full of verses speaking only about friends. We are told that a friend loves at all times. This means in the good times and the not so good times, **Proverbs 17:17a**. Oil and perfume make the heart glad, and the sweetness of a friend comes from his earnest counsel (**Proverbs 27:9**).

Something else I've learned about friendships, most of them take time and effort, and this is on both parties. The greater the investment in a friendship, the greater the return on that investment. I have a formula that goes like this: An acquaintance + invested time = friend. A friend + invested time = good friend. A good friend + in vested time = best friend and it's this kind of friend that you can share your deepest secrets with and know they will not be violated.

Norma and I are truly blessed because many of our best friends came about when God supernaturally intervened and we went from an acquaintance to a true and faithful best friend almost overnight; we know that it was God and we are convinced that God is truly the giver of good gifts; our best friends are our most precious and good gifts to us from our heavenly Father.

One last thing, a real true friend will encourage you to become more than you think you can become and will almost always challenge you to get closer to God and develop a true intimacy with Jesus. A true friend will always see the good in you and will not put you down, but challenge you by lifting you up.

We are told there is no greater love than to lay down one's life for one's friends. (**John 15:13**). We are also told no longer do I call you servants, for the servant does not know what his master is doing; but I have called you friends, for all that I have heard from my Father I have made known to you (**John 15:15**).

The good news is we all have one true and best friend that can really be counted on and in all times and He is a friend that sticks closer than a brother, a friend that loves at all times, a friend that is the way, and the truth, and the life, a friend that if we confess our sins, he is faithful and just to forgive us our sins and to cleanse us from all unrighteousness, a friend that will never leave you nor forsake you.

He's not only a friend we can boast about, but someone we can even sing about as we hear these words: What a friend we have in Jesus, All our sins and griefs to bear! What a privilege to carry everything to God in prayer! Oh, what peace we often forfeit, Oh, what needless pain we bear, All because we do not carry everything to God in prayer!

Prayer: Lord, you've told me in your word that you no longer call me a servant, but a friend. Teach me how to truly enter in to a friendship relationship with you at all times.

1. Do you really believe that the Lord is your friend that sticks closer than a brother? Why?

Week 46
Your Declaration Will Be Heard

I was sitting here looking out the window and just letting my mind wander where I believe God was directing my thoughts. Notice I didn't say aimless wanderings, but directed wanderings. He took me to a place where I was thinking about the confessions or declarations that people make, both knowingly and unknowingly.

What exactly are confessions or declarations? They sound like they would be the same thing. A confession is an affirmation or acknowledgement and a declaration is a confirmation or a decree.

So what comes out of our mouths isn't just a bunch of meaningless words with no substance and no basis for their utterance. When we confess or declare something, it is for all realism, an affirmation, acknowledgement, a confirmation or decree of something that we assume is completely and totally true in our lives.

On the flip side of that thinking, why would anyone confess or declare something that is not true, we know that as a lie or a statement based on untrue facts or false information. Either way, it's a shame on you situation for not researching the facts prior to making it a declaration of a truth that is for all practical purposes not true at all.

Why am I beating this to death so to speak? Because I've seen so many people do the wrong thing so many times that it almost seems to be the right and natural thing to do or

215

say. I've seen so many people confess and declare to something that is so incorrect and they have done it so many times that it seems to be the right thing to do.

Here's an example: God who cannot lie tells us in **Philippians 4:13,** that I can do all things through him who strengthens me and yet we declare we can't do this or we can't do that or I'll never be able to do anything and we make our declaration an acknowledgement or confirmation of something that is not true and a lie and probably based upon our feelings or what we think is a lack of ability.

Here's another example of our faulty confessions: The same God who cannot lie tells us in **Deuteronomy 28:13,** and the Lord will make you the head and not the tail, and you shall only go up and not down, and yet, so many confess with an absolute certainty that they are a loser or a no-body and going nowhere in life and they make this confession or acknowledgement based on their present circumstances in life as if where they are or where they were is all there is to life.

I don't know about you, but my God is a God of hope. My God tells me: may the God of hope fill you with all joy and peace in believing, so that by the power of the Holy Spirit you may abound in hope (**Romans 15:13**), He also says to me; "For I know the plans I have for you, declares the Lord, plans for welfare and not for evil, to give you a future and a hope" (**Jeremiah 29:11**).

Now, I know that most people want to please the Lord and do exactly what He wants us to do. I can't imagine anyone knowingly saying or doing something that is not pleasing to God. If we are careful of what we say in front of a judge or a group of people, why can't we be careful in front of an all knowing God? We know that **Psalm 19:14** tells us; let the words of my mouth and the meditation of my heart be acceptable in your sight, O Lord, my rock and my redeemer, and yet the words of our mouth which is really our confession or declaration of where we think we are is actually filled with negative words and think that they will be acceptable in God's sight.

How can they be acceptable in God's sight when they are totally and completely contrary to what God has to say about you? God says you are a winner and you tell Him you are a loser. God says you can do all things through Christ and you tell him you can't do anything. God says you are a somebody and you tell Him you are a nobody and yet you believe that He is pleased with your negative declarations.

You see, my friend, your declarations will be heard. If faith comes through hearing, how much more will fear come through hearing? It's almost as if you're fighting God in order to convince yourself that what you are saying is a fact and by your constant negative confessions about yourself that somehow God will agree with you. That, my friend, will never happen. God will never agree with your negative declarations about yourself because God cannot lie and will not agree to something that is contrary to His faithful word. By the way contrary means; conflicting or opposing or disagreeing.

In other words, God will never agree to something that is a lie regardless of how much you may think it's true. It would be a lot easier for you to change your way of thinking than it would be to ask God to go against His very own word. It's easier for you to change your mind than for God to change His ways.

Here's another truth you need to think about; your negative confessions will never put a smile on God's face nor will it bring you any joy. Your negative declarations about yourself or others are not statements of truth, but a form of complaints and whining. If you can complain about it, you can pray about it.

Sometimes, we misquote scripture especially in the book **1 Thessalonians 5:17** which tells us to "Pray without ceasing" and we interpret it to mean whine without ceasing or complain without ceasing. Often times, we do it so often that we confuse the new wine with the new whine. Just to be clear, one is a delightful, fruit oriented drink and the other is complaining and moaning. One is pleasing and was used by our Lord; the other is never pleasing and was never used by our Lord.

I believe and declare that you are a new creation in Christ Jesus and that includes your mind, the way you think, and the words that come out of your mouth, and that you will begin from this day on to agree with every promise that God has declared over your life, your family, your situations, your finances and your health.

I proclaim that you no longer have to look for a weapon to defeat the enemy, but that you realize that you are the weapon in the hands of an Almighty God that does not know the word defeat, you are a ruthless giant killer in the name of Jesus.

Prayer: Father, I know that you are the Lord God Almighty and your presence extends to the eternal past, present and the eternal future and your word is established in heaven and will never change. Teach me to open my mouth and proclaim and declare to others who you are in my life.

1. Do you sometimes get nervous about declaring the word of God to non-believers? Why?
2. Are there times when you get all excited about events, celebrations, sports activities, but deep down you would like to get that excited about the Lord? What's stopping you?

Week 47
You Put it to Death

During my devotional this morning, I was taken to Romans chapters 7 and 8, but verse 13 of chapter 8 really jumped off the page.

I'm told, if you live by your corrupt nature, you are going to die. But if you use your spiritual nature to put to death the evil activities of the body, you will live (**Romans 8:13**).

I guess a good question would be, what is a corrupt nature or as many versions put it, what is the sin nature?

The sin nature is that attitude in man that makes him rebellious against God, so when we speak of the sin nature, we're referring to the fact that we have a natural disposition or character to sin, Truth be told, when given the choice to do God's will or our own, we will naturally choose to do our own thing.

When given the choice, we would rather be on the throne of our own lives, in control of our own decisions and the center of our own universe. Submission is something that doesn't come natural to the sinful nature.

You might not be fully convinced, but evidence of the sin nature flourishes. No one has to teach a child to lie or be selfish; as a matter of fact, we go to great lengths to teach children to tell the truth and put others first. Sinful behavior comes naturally.

You might not like to admit it, but wherever people are, there is trouble, just listen to the news. Charles Spurgeon said, "As the salt flavors every drop in the Atlantic Ocean, so does sin affect every atom of our nature.

This is not a teaching to convince you of what you already know, namely our sinful nature. The Word of God explains the reason for the suffering; basically, humanity is sinful and not just in theory or in practice, but by its very nature. Sin is part of the very fiber of our being and who we are. The stain runs deep—it's in the existence and make-up of our souls.

Sometimes, its very existence amazes me when I read scripture. The story of the flood for example. We're told the Lord saw how great the wickedness of the human race had become on the earth, and that every inclination of the thoughts of the human heart was only evil all the time. The Lord regretted that he had made human beings on the earth, and his heart was deeply troubled. So the Lord said, "I will wipe from the face of the earth the human race I have created—and with them the animals, the birds and the creatures that move along the ground—for I regret that I have made them." But Noah found favor in the eyes of the Lord (**Genesis 6:5-8**).

We all know the story, how it rained and everything on the earth, under the earth and above the earth was destroyed except for Noah and his sons, Shem, Ham and Japheth, together with his wife and the wives of his three sons, entered the ark. I can count all that remained on the planet earth on my two hands and that would be 8 people. Yet, with only 8 people on the entire planet, the sinful nature of man was still present in each and every one of them. Even if there were only two people on the earth, the truth is the sin nature is universal in humanity. All of us have a sinful nature, and it affects every part of us. This is what's called the doctrine of total depravity, and it's biblical. All of us have gone astray (**Isaiah 53:6**).

Back to our original verse, if you live by your corrupt nature, you are going to die. But if you use your spiritual nature to put to death the evil activities of the body, you will live (Romans 8:13).

Wouldn't it be great if God Himself killed the sinful nature in us and we didn't have to do anything? I mean wouldn't it be really nice if the rebelliousness, the pride, the arrogance, the stealing, the lying and everything that puts us at odds with God were somehow just gone. It would be nice, but as they say; don't hold your breath. This is why Romans tells us; but if you use your spiritual nature to put to death the evil activities of the body.

We are told you put it to death; you do it yourself with the help of your spiritual nature. This is called a battle. One nature fighting against another nature and all wrapped up in one body, namely, yours. One nature your spiritual sends a heads up that something is wrong and it's coming from your sinful nature and it tells you that you must kill it, destroy it, get rid of it.

Think of it this way: we have a body system that helps fight off sickness and it's called the immune system. The immune system is made up of a network of cells, tissues, and organs that work together to protect the body. In this system are white blood cells, which are part of this defense system. There are two basic types of these germ-fighting cells, one that chews up invading germs and another that allows the body to remember and recognize previous invaders.

This is how the spiritual nature helps us fight off the invaders of the sinful nature and allows us to remember and recognize the previous invaders, so when those sinful thoughts come back, we know where they come from and we are able to take control of our thoughts and actions and put them to death through the blood of Jesus.

Put it to death? What do you mean by that? I mean you don't agree with it, you don't want it, need it or accept it and you defeat it or you become victorious by not giving in to its demands. The spiritual nature gives you a spiritual heads up that this thought or desire is a no-no and is not pleasing to your heavenly Father. It's telling you that it comes from your sin nature and its hostility toward God and ignorance of His truth.

Is it easy to put to death the temptations, demands or desires of the sinful nature? Of course not, that's why it's called a battle and the good news is you don't have to try to defeat it in your own strength, wisdom or cleverness, but by using your spiritual nature, you can do it, let me repeat that; You Can Do It, and please stop asking God to do what He has already asked you to do.

We don't lose our sin nature once we receive Christ. The Bible says that sin remains in us and that a struggle with that old nature will continue as long as we are in this world.

Here's some great news concerning our daily battle. We have help in the battle—divine help. The Spirit of God takes up residence in each believer and supplies the power we need to overcome the demands of the sin nature within us. "No one born of God makes a practice of sinning, for God's seed abides in him, and he cannot keep on sinning because he has been born of God" (**1 John 3:9**).

Through the finished work on the cross, Jesus Christ satisfied God's anger against sin and provided believers with victory over their sin nature: "He himself bore our sins' in his body on the cross, so that we might die to sins and live for righteousness" (**1 Peter 2:24**). In His resurrection, Jesus offers life to everyone bound by corrupt flesh. Those who are born again now have this command: "Count yourselves dead to sin but alive to God in Christ Jesus.

Prayer: Lord, I know that sin separates me from you, please help me to be careful with my decisions and choices in life that I might not sin against you in word or in deed.

1. If you don't like the fruits of sin, stay out of the devils orchard. What does that mean to you?
2. In the eyes of the Lord do you think there is a difference between a big sin and a little sin? Does it make any difference to you?

Week 48
Let's be Real

Today's sharing is going to be a little different. I'm going to use a lot of humor and examples in order to make a point. I really hope you enjoy it.

The other day I was reading in **Psalm 73:2-5, 12,** which really caught my attention. "But as for me, my feet had almost slipped; I had nearly lost my foothold. For I envied the arrogant when I saw the prosperity of the wicked. They have no struggles; their bodies are healthy and strong. They are free from common human burdens; they are not plagued by human ills. This is what the wicked are like. Always free of care, they go on amassing wealth."

Another version says it this way: But my feet had almost stumbled. They had almost slipped because I was envious of arrogant people when I saw the prosperity that wicked people enjoy.

Granted, the verses are speaking about arrogant or wicked people, but as the title of this message indicates, let's be real. How many times have we been envious when we see the prosperity of others? Example, when we watch on the news the newborns of the royalty born in England. Sure, it always starts out, oh how cute, or aren't they adorable or what beautiful children. Without even trying, a thought always enters that says; those children are set for life or they will never have to work a day in their life or those kids got it made.

It would almost seem that human nature is envious of the prosperity of others. How true it is when we are told in **Ephesians 6:12a,** for we do not wrestle against flesh and blood. Envy is a real problem, especially the type that sneaks into our thoughts and catches us by surprise. What exactly is envy or to be envious? It's defined as a feeling of discontent or covetousness with regard to another's advantages, success or possessions. The advanced English Dictionary defines it as a desire to have something that is possessed by another or a painful or resentful awareness of an awareness enjoyed by another joined with a desire to possess the same advantage.

It's not a vicious or constant nagging or desire for the possessions but gosh, wouldn't it be nice or thoughts of what if.

Isn't it interesting, it doesn't say that we want to be the other person, but to just have their advantage or possessions in life. As I thought about that, it became very clear that statement is very accurate indeed. Example, Mike Tyson the boxer had accumulated over 240 million dollars in his boxing career. Of course, the last time they interviewed him not to long ago, he had less than $100.00 to his name. No one said I really wish I was Mike Tyson. What many said is I really wish I had all his money so I could take it easy in life. Many people are not envious of the person just the possessions. Still, somewhere in the back of our mind, we still wonder what it would be like to have their wealth regardless of verses like **Proverbs 23:17,** let not your heart envy sinners, but continue in the fear of the Lord all the day or **Proverbs 24:19,** agonize not yourself because of evildoers, and be not envious of the wicked.

I think it's almost comical some of the thoughts or comments people have concerning the very wealthy. A good friend of mine told me the story of how a number of church goers went to the home of a very, very wealthy person to do some yard work. This was a million dollar home with pool and tennis courts and amazing yardwork. One of the people in the group said; I bet with all this wealth and amazing home that the owner is probably really not a very happy person. Almost without blinking an eye one of the other group members commented; God, I hope so.

We all realize that **Deuteronomy 8:18,** you shall remember the Lord your God, for it is he who gives you power to get wealth is absolutely true, yet we often think to ourselves, a little wealth couldn't hurt, could it Lord? Kind of reminds me of the cartoon of Father Faber. He's looking up to heaven and says; God, I know you have a mansion for me in heaven, but couldn't I have the mansion here on earth and a two bedroom one bath in heaven?

While living in Florida, I heard a story and I'm not sure if it's absolutely true or not, but it helps to make a point, of a visiting preacher that was going to speak at this large church. One of the congregation members who was a very wealthy business person was going to pick up the guest speaker at the airport and drive him to the church. The speaker is waiting outside the terminal and a brand new, very large Mercedes drives up and the speaker gets in the car and off they go. After a few minutes, the speaker asks the driver what he does a living, to which the man replies, I own things. A few seconds go by and the guest speaker asks, what do you own? Not wanting to seem boastful, the business man says, see that shopping center, I own that. See that hotel, I own that too, I also own that office building and that car dealership and that strip mall just to name a few things. The speaker really amazed says, my God, I wouldn't know what to do with all those things to which the businessman says, and that's why the Lord didn't give them to you, I know exactly what to do with them to bring glory to the Lord.

I remember once the lottery went up to 84 million dollars. I told myself, this is a great opportunity to seriously start seeking God for a miracle. I even tried to bargain with God and told Him, Lord if you let me win this lottery, I will give you half. Lord can you imagine what I could do for your kingdom with half of the lottery? I even said; God, give me one good reason why I shouldn't win? After a few moments, I heard in my spirit; because if I let you win the lottery, it would destroy our relationship and I wouldn't see you again. After a few moments and not giving up on the idea of winning, I asked the Lord, okay, how much can I win and still have a pretty good relationship? To which I heard in my spirit, son, don't go there.

What's the secret when you have not been born with a fortune or have not been able to make millions in your life? For me, the answer is always to be found in the word of God.

Hebrews 13:5, keep your life free from the love of money, and be content with what you have, for he has said, "I will never leave you nor forsake you." Again, in **1 Timothy 6:8,** but if we have food and clothing, with these we will be content.

What does it mean to be content? It means to be satisfied or showing satisfaction with things as they are. You see my friends, if we can't be content with who the Lord made us to be or with what He has given us, we will never be content with anything else. For a believer being content with who and what you are is seeking His face, wanting bigger and better things in life is seeking His hand.

Prayer: Father, you created me just the way I am and in your eyes I am perfect. Help me to see myself and others through your eyes that I may not have a judgmental, critical spirit.

1. Are you happy with the way God made you or do you sometimes feel like he could have done better?
2. What really makes you happy and content? Why?
3. Do you ever envy others that seem to have it all together?
4. Do you really believe the grass is greener in the other field?

Week 49
You Are Not Alone

You know, when I was a teenager growing up in New York and coming from a family of two older brothers and two younger sisters, Looking back over many of the things I did, I'm amazed how I thought that every wrong thing I did would never be seen or known by my Mom or my brothers and how I didn't care if my sisters found out because my philosophy was mine is always right and my sisters wouldn't dare turn me in or else they knew what would happen to them. It's not that I did evil things; it's just that some of the things were very mischievous and besides, if I did get caught, I could always blame my sisters.

When I got older, in college, I outgrew that behavior only to take on another behavior that was just as bad. If I did something wrong, I would take on the ostrich syndrome. If there was a situation, figuratively speaking, I'd just bury my head in the sand and make believe it didn't exist and that eventually it would go away. Many times the issue did go away for me, but someone else usually suffered some degree of the consequence of my behavior.

Many of us do that today within the church. We either see something or know about something that needs to be addressed like a brother or sister in need or a family that has no food to feed their children or no money to buy clothes and we turn our heads the other way which is no different than sticking our heads in the sand and hoping the need goes away or we spiritualize the situation and tell ourselves it's not my ministry or I don't have a green light.

You see, my friend, our decisions for anything, are never just ours alone. Every situation we find ourselves is never a situation where we are all alone. I was reading in **Proverbs 5:21**. For a man's ways are before the eyes of the Lord, and He ponders all his paths. Another word for ponder is to think about or consider. Another way to phrase this is **Hebrews 4:13,** nothing in all creation is hidden from God's sight. Everything is uncovered and laid bare before the eyes of him to whom we must give account. Granted, we can always fall back on **I John 1:9** if we confess our sins, he is faithful and just to forgive us our sins and to cleanse us from all unrighteousness and God is faithful to forgive us, but there's still consequences for our actions, even something as simple as turning our heads on a needy brother or sister.

You might be asking yourself; what kind of consequences could there possibly be?

Here's an example of not being obedient and the consequences that followed. Many years ago when I was living in Puerto Rico, I was in the mall and a young boy in a wheel chair who was being pushed by an adult came right by me and I clearly heard the Lord say; lay hands on him and I will raise him up. Being afraid of failing, I said no and walked to another part of the mall. Within 30 minutes, this same young boy came right by me and I heard the Lord say the same thing, lay hands on him and I will raise him up. A second time, I said no and walked away. This happened four times where I said no. What were the consequences of my action? A missed opportunity to see

God raise a young boy out of a wheel chair and set him free from his bondage that kept him confined to a wheel chair. That missed opportunity can never be recovered by me. Was I alone in this decision? Of course not, we are never alone in anything we do, whether it is righteous or sinful. Even, our deepest thoughts are not ours to do with as we see fit and our silent thoughts on earth are broadcasted very loudly in heaven by He who knows our every thought.

By the very nature of being alive, we have become accountable to God for everything we do. Once again **Proverbs 5:21**, for a man's ways are before the eyes of the Lord, and He ponders all his paths. Which ways are before the Lord? Every way, every trip, every journey that we take in life is being watched by the Lord. If it were not so, why would it tell us in **Job 34:21** His eyes are on the ways of mortals; he sees their every step.

Why would God have to ponder our ways, doesn't He know the ending from the beginning? I personally believe it's for the same reason that we often go before God and say to Him that we want to be honest with Him. It's not that God is waiting for us to be honest or that He has to watch our very steps because He has no clue what our next step is. It's because God want us to come to that place that we realize our every thought, our every step, our every action is known by God and that we should use wisdom in all that we do and come to that place that everything we do will be done out of obedience to God and that our life's goal is to be pleasing to God in all that we do even as we are told in **Colossians 3:17** and whatever you do or say, do it as a representative of the Lord Jesus, giving thanks through him to God the Father.

As a representative of the Lord Jesus Christ, how can I give thanks to the Father by hiding my head in the sand hoping a situation will go away or how can I thank the Father by saying no to His Son in setting a young boy free from his wheel chair. How can I be a representative of Jesus Christ in thinking I'm all alone in any decision that needs to be made? Truth be told, when we think we are alone in anything that we do, we deny the word of God that tells us in **Hebrews 13:5,** God has said, Never will I leave you; never will I forsake you.

My friend, we are never alone and our actions are always before the eyes of our Father in heaven.

Prayer: Lord, I know you tell me I am never alone, but sometimes that's exactly how I feel, alone. Help me not to live my life based on my feelings, but upon what your holy word tells me.

1. What's the difference between being alone and being lonely? Do you ever experience either? What do you do when that happens?
2. Is it possible to be lonely in the midst of a crowd? Why?

WEEK 50

Hey! Where's My Package?

Christmas can be such a time of stress. It can be stressful even if you're not doing anything, just watching everyone else get stressed out. Even if you just go to the mall at the last moment and watch the buyers running around. It almost looks like someone kicked an ant's nest and they all scatter. I think stress can be contagious.

Anyway, I was watching Norma at the table the other day, wrapping lots of little packages and it brought to my mind an incident I had many years ago which triggered this sharing with you.

I was expecting a package from UPS and it was late, at least by two days, I mean I already received a notice saying it would be delivered on a specific date and that date had already passed. I called UPS and said, "Hey, where's my package?" They checked all the detail and said we left it at your house. Well, where did you leave it, I asked, in the front of the house or the back of the house because I don't have my package and I need it. They said it was left in the front of the house behind some bushes to keep it safe.

I immediately went to check it out and there was my package exactly where they said they left it. Although it was hidden and out of sight, it was still there. I just needed some clarification as to exactly where it was left. I thought it would be right in front of the door in plain sight like the TV commercials show us.

234

It brought to mind a scripture from **John 14:27,** that tells us: Peace I leave with you, My peace I give to you; not as the world gives do I give to you..." In other words, Jesus says I'm leaving you with a package. It's a package of peace and not just any peace, but My peace.

Thank God for His gifts. Jesus says I'm leaving you with peace and I'm trying to figure out why I'm in pieces. So the other day I'm speaking to the Lord and I asked with reverence to the King of Kings hey, where's my package of peace? Did you leave it at the front of the house or the back of the house because for sure I didn't receive it and I don't have it? Now, I knew according to **Philippians 4:7** that the peace of God surpasses all understanding and I also knew that according to **Isaiah 9:6,** it was the Prince of Peace Himself that gave me His peace.

So, the Lord says it's in your heart according to My Word. I checked it out in **Colossians 3:15** just to be sure because I couldn't find my package. I mean at this point I wasn't really too interested in multiplied peace as it tells me in **2 Peter 1:2**, all I wanted was the basic package of peace to make it through this stressful moment.

The Lord told me, "You have too many bushes or things in your heart and that's why you can't find it. And by the way, He continued, My peace is not just for the stressful moment but for the rest of your life."

Wow, I thought; for the rest of my life. At that moment, I began to go over in my mind the many teachings and messages that I taught or preached about the peace of God.

I remembered that the peace of God is not a thing, but a person and that person has a name and that name is Jesus. I remembered that Prince of Peace said I will never leave you or forget you, which is different from my forgetting Him for a short time.

You know, it's amazing the things you remember when you take the time to think about the things you've said and take the time to remember them. Bushes or things in the heart or the mind can be a terrible thing because they hide the things that are so important to life and how you live it.

So I began to rationalize to myself, or self-talk as we are so often accustomed to do when things seem out of kilter; and I thought; Jesus is in my heart and He is my peace. At this very moment, I am not experiencing peace which means someone stole my peace or I let someone replace my peace with stress. If someone stole it, then it had to be a thief. I remembered **John 10:10** where the Lord reminded me that the enemy is a thief and "the thief does not come except to steal and to kill, and to destroy." Another version says it this way: The thief comes only to steal and kill and destroy.

I thought about it and realized that the enemy snuck in, stole my peace, killed my joy and destroyed my peaceful stability. There's an old British and American saying, you can't see the woods for the trees. What it means is; someone is unable to understand what is important in a situation because they are giving too much attention to details.

I was so focused on the stressful situation that I failed to see the truth of what the Lord was saying and I needed to back up and see the whole picture. In other words, there were too many bushes getting in the way of what was really important. Once I did that, I was able to see clearly the tactics of the enemy and victory was in sight and assured. Stress had to bow its knee to the Lordship of Jesus Christ and it had to flee.

You know, the tactics of the enemy are really not that hidden. They are out and in the open. The reason we can't see them is we often have too many bushes that conceal them.

So for this Christmas season, my friend, know this, peace is ours and so is joy, and love, and victory, and all the spiritual blessings in the heavenly places in Christ according to **Ephesians 1:3**.

Prayer: Father, I know you have given me your peace, so help me to live in peace and not pieces.

1. If the Lord has given you His peace, are you walking in it or have you given it away?
2. **Do** you think it's possible to experience a life filled with the peace of God? How can you justify your answer?

Week 51

Just Follow the Instructions

This is a very special time of the year and one that I personally really enjoy, Christmas. I love the music, the lights, the colorful decorations and just about everything associated with the reason for the season. I enjoy going to friends' homes and the wonderful smells coming from their kitchens as they prepare festive meals and I really enjoy the anticipation that lingers in the air. There's no getting away from it, there's something special about Christmas and the Christmas season.

There's even something special about telling people, Merry Christmas and not just happy holidays, after all, there is a reason for the season. If we can say happy birthday or happy anniversary or even happy New Year, then we can say Merry Christmas.

Well, not to get side-tracked, but Christmas is also about gifts and for many, with these gifts come instructions. What exactly are instructions? Well, they are directions or guidelines or even recommendations on how to do something. In most cases, these directions or guidelines are proven steps to get a desired end results that works the way the product was intended to work and without any glitches, problems or malfunctions.

Granted, sometimes it would seem the instructions were put together by someone who seems to have gotten lost in the fog and never found their way back to earth, but if you just follow the instructions, the end product should put a smile

238

on the face of the person receiving the gift. Notice I said sometimes. It really depends on whether you followed the instructions as intended or not.

Many, many years ago I bought a bike for my daughter and I looked at the instructions and convinced myself that I could do it faster and easier without the instructions. By the time I was done, the bike looked great, really great. The only problem was the front wheel wouldn't move. It was tightly fastened and wouldn't turn and besides that, I had many extra parts from the assembly of the front wheel. The back wheel turned great, but the front wheel was locked in place. You don't have to be a rocket scientist to realize that if the front tire doesn't turn, the bike isn't going anyplace. I wasn't about to give my daughter a brand new bike and tell her, Merry Christmas, here's your bike, it's new and pretty and colorful, but there's just one minor problem, it doesn't work, the front tire doesn't spin. Solution. Take the bike apart, and start over and just follow the instructions.

You know, there are instructions for just about everything in life and so often we think we can re-write the instructions hoping to save time. What we end up with is the expression, I didn't have time to do it right the first time, but I made time to do it right the second time. Why? Because we followed the proven, tried instructions.

Even the bible tells us what the name means. BIBLE: basic instructions before leaving earth.

Sometimes, instructions can be more forceful and given with an authority that leaves the follower with very little choice in what they need to do, and we call those instructions a command.

When a police officer tells you to roll your window down, pull your car over to the side of the road and wait in the car, he's given you instructions what to do with your car and you don't have any choice in what and how to do it, because those instructions come in the form of a command.

We are given instructions every day. Practical, physical, mental and even spiritual instructions. The good news is when we follow the instructions as directed; we usually have a happy ending, even if we don't like the instructions or the person giving the instructions.

Do you remember the old poster that said: God said it, I believe it, that settles it? I realized that the sign was wrong and should have said: God said it, that settles it. Why was the original sign wrong? Because in my personal opinion, what I believe doesn't change what God said, only my relationship to what God said and what God said is always the truth.

In other words, God's instructions for my life are always much better than what I think or feel about how my life should be lived. For one thing, God knows the ending from the beginning, which means He already knows the outcome for my life, so when God tells me in **Proverbs 3:5,6** …trust in the LORD with all your heart and do not lean on your own understanding. In all your ways, acknowledge Him, and He will make your paths straight.

In other words, God is telling us, these are the instructions for your life. Trust in Me and not your feelings or the pitter-patter of your heart because your heart can really fool you and don't lean on your own understanding, your wealth, your education, your gut-feelings or your past experiences. In everything you do, recognize Me, God, and I will direct your steps through this life which is a mine-field.

We may look at **Proverbs 3:5, 6** and call them bible verses, but let's call it what it really is, instructions from God on how to live our lives.

You might be asking yourself; does God actually give us instructions? You know He does. In **Genesis 26:5,** we read, I will do this because Abraham listened to me and obeyed all my requirements, commands, decrees, and instructions." My friends, the entire bible is filled with instructions that God gives us to live a freer, healthier, happier, more productive life and one that is filled with the blessings of heaven because God blesses obedience.

Have you ever noticed or maybe even been guilty yourself of not obeying God's instructions and we get into a big mess? What do we do? We blame God for not coming through or we blame our spouse or our children or our family or our friends or boss, or Mother Nature or the enemy or just about anyone or everyone except ourselves for not following the instructions. And what is God telling us? Just follow the instructions.

How many have heard about the gift that keeps on giving? It's called obedience or just following God's instructions.

I leave you with this thought, in **Isaiah 46:10,** we are told from the beginning I revealed the end. From long ago, I told you things that had not yet happened, saying, "My plan will stand, and I'll do everything I intended to do." Meaning that God truly knows the ending from the beginning and when He says He will direct our paths, He means He has the best instructions for our lives and He will not lead us in to failure or disaster or disappointment, but has the best plans for our lives and all we have to do is realize that He is in control of all our out of controls and just follow His instructions because God has never failed us, is not failing us now and has no plans to fail you in the future, He is faithful to a thousand generations.

Prayer: Oh God, when you give me instructions on life, help me to be teachable and open minded knowing that you have only the best for me and love me just as I am.

1. Do you find following God's instructions for life to make sense to you all the time? Do you still follow them anyway?
2. If God knows the ending from the beginning, does it make any sense to follow your own instructions and directions for life? Regardless if you said yes or no, justify your answer

WEEK 52
Now That Christmas Is Over

Can you believe it, another year is just days away? As a matter-of-fact, this will be the last message of this year. Where does the time fly? For Norma and me, it has been an amazing roller coaster ride. We've been to Israel twice had many new adventures that showed us that God is still on the throne and in control of all the out of controls, and He is not running for re-election, thank God.

The following mini-devotional is for you to think about as we leave one year and enter another year and as we leave the festive Christmas season behind us. A lot like when you go on a trip, and as the plane takes off, you look out the window and see your familiar surroundings begin to get smaller and smaller until they disappear and are gone and out of sight.

Well, now that Christmas is over and all the packages are opened and being enjoyed, we can rest a little more easily. Do you remember that special joyful feeling you had as the unopened gift was handed to you? There was joy, anticipation and excitement because you had no idea what the gift contained. I'm sure some of you peeked or had an idea, but I mean the gifts that came unexpected and you had no idea what was beneath the colorful wrappings. Be truthful now, there really was an excitement and an anticipation to open the gift. What went through your head? You probably thought it could be a Rolex watch or that piece of electronic equipment that you personally would have never bought but dropped enough hints to everyone; everywhere that you would have really, really liked it. Remember we're being real. Can you imagine if someone gave you a gift that kept on giving every day of your life? Talk about a gift. Wow! That would be an incredible gift; can you really imagine a gift that would keep on giving every day of your life?

Imagine a battery that would always be at 100% and never wear down no matter how much you used it or a line of credit that no matter how much you used it, it was always full or a checking account that no matter how many checks you made the account was always exceedingly, abundantly full.

Well, here's the good news, someone actually did give you a gift that keeps on giving every day of your life. The word of God tells me in **John 3:16,** 'For God so loved the world that he gave a gift that would keep giving every single day of your life; that gift was a person and that person has a name, also, that gift needs to be unwrapped and enjoyed because he brings with Him peace and joy and contentment and love.

Sometimes, it's hard to think of a person as a gift, but the word give here in **John 3:16** is the Greek word "didomi" and it means to give something to someone or to give to the one asking or to supply or furnish even if one is not asking.

How does this apply to us? Well, the Father gave something to not only someone, but to everyone.

Like that gift you received for Christmas, you had no idea what was inside it until you took off the wrappings. Once that happened, you were either very surprised and either happy or disappointed, not very surprised and neutral or could care less because it wasn't something that you wanted or needed. The point being you had no idea until the gift was unwrapped.

Well, it's the same thing with the gift the Father gave us. Oh, you might be happy when you first received it, but that was a superficial happiness because you had and still have no idea the depth of the gift that keeps on giving.

This could be a very lengthy sharing, but to keep it on the short side, here are just a few things that this Gift keeps on giving to us all the days of our life:

John 12:44-46. A way out of darkness -- "I have come as light into the world, that everyone who believes in Me may not remain in darkness."

John 6:32-35. Satisfaction, an end to our inner thirst -- Jesus therefore said to them, "Truly, truly, I say to you, it is not Moses who has given you the bread out of heaven, but it is My Father who gives you the true bread out of heaven. For the bread of God is that which comes down out of heaven, and gives life to the world." They said therefore to Him, "Lord, evermore give us this bread." Jesus said to them, "I am the bread of life; he who comes to Me shall not hunger, and he who believes in Me shall never thirst."

245

John 8:12. Direction in life -- Again therefore Jesus spoke to them, saying, "I am the light of the world; he who follows Me shall not walk in the darkness, but shall have the light of life."

Matthew 20:25-28 and Mark 9:31-32. Payment for our sin -- "The Son of Man did not come to be served, but to serve, and to give His life a ransom for many." He was teaching His disciples and telling them, "The Son of Man is to be delivered into the hands of men, and they will kill Him; and when He has been killed, He will rise three days later." But they did not understand this statement, and they were afraid to ask Him.

John 10:7-11. Abundant life -- Jesus therefore said to them again, "Truly, truly, I say to you, I am the door of the sheep. All who came before Me are thieves and robbers, but the sheep did not hear them. I am the door; if anyone enters through Me, he shall be saved, and shall go in and out, and find pasture. The thief comes only to steal, and kill, and destroy; I came that they might have life, and might have it abundantly. I am the good shepherd; the good shepherd lays down His life for the sheep."

Mark 2:3-12. Forgiveness of sin -- Some men came, bringing to him a paralytic, carried by four of them. Since they could not get him to Jesus because of the crowd, they made an opening in the roof above Jesus and, after digging through it, lowered the mat the paralyzed man was lying on. When Jesus saw their faith, he said to the paralytic, "Son, your sins are forgiven." Now some teachers of the law were sitting there, thinking to themselves, "Why does this fellow talk like that? He's blaspheming! Who can forgive sins but God alone?" Immediately, Jesus knew in his spirit that this was what they were thinking in their hearts, and he said to them, "Why are you thinking these things? Which is easier: to say to the paralytic, 'Your sins are forgiven,' or to say, 'Get up, take your mat and walk'? But that you may know that the Son of Man has authority on earth to forgive sins...' He said to the paralytic, "I tell you, get up, take your mat and go home." He got up, took his mat and walked out in full view of them all. This amazed everyone and they praised God, saying, "We have never seen anything like this!"

John 6:37-40. Eternal life -- "All that the Father gives Me shall come to Me, and the one who comes to Me I will certainly not cast out. For I have come down from heaven, not to do My own will, but the will of Him who sent Me. And this is the will of Him who sent Me, that of all that He has given Me I lose nothing, but raise it up on the last day. For this is the will of My Father, that everyone who beholds the Son and believes in Him, may have eternal life; and I Myself will raise him up on the last day."

So my friends, as we enter the New Year, let's not think that the gifts are gone and Christmas is over and it's T-minus, however, many days until next holiday or long weekend, we have a gift called Jesus that was given to us by His Father and our heavenly Father so we can enjoy Him all the days of our life and this gift will never leave us nor forsake us and it's new every morning just like the mercies of God.

Prayer: Father, help me to realize that the gift you gave me in your Son is not a one-time gift, but a gift that keeps on giving and never stops or gets old.

1. Since God has given you a wonderful gift called Jesus, have you unwrapped the gift so you can enjoy the blessings of the gift all year long?
2. What is the benefit of having a gift if you never unwrap it or put it to use? Would you agree it's like having medication but never using it? Why would you do that?

ABOUT THE AUTHOR

Even as a young boy, Don Honig knew that there was always something that was much bigger in life, but had a hard time trying to understand what it was.

Growing up in New York City in a Jewish home, things of a spiritual nature were not encouraged and asking questions about the Lord Jesus Christ was definitely frowned upon and strictly unmentionable in the home.

Much later in life, Don tried to disprove many of the deeds that Jesus Christ claimed, and in order to do that, Don started to read the bible, Old and New Covenant. The Old Covenant was somewhat familiar with many of the names of the individuals found there, but the New Covenant became a real challenge, and eventually, Don was faced with a major crisis. He either had to accept or deny the many claims that Jesus made. The dilemma was, all the claims were true and Don couldn't deny the truth and had no choice but to joyfully accept the Jewish Messiah as his personal Lord and Savior.

It is the desire of Don Honig to speak the Word of God through the power of the Holy Spirit and to see the captives set free, the blind receive their sight and the deaf hear the good news.

Don will continue by the leading and guiding of the Lord to bring people out of darkness and death into God's glorious light and life through the Word of God with demonstrations of signs and wonders.

Made in the USA
Middletown, DE
18 April 2017